FUNDRAISING FOR THE SMALL PUBLIC LIBRARY

A How-To-Do-It Manual
for Librarians

JAMES SWAN

NEAL-SCHUMAN PUBLISHERS, INC.
New York, London   1990

Published by Neal-Schuman Publishers, Inc.
23 Leonard Street
New York, NY 10013

Copyright © 1990 by Neal-Schuman Publishers, Inc.

Printed and bound in the United States of America

Library of Congress Cataloging-in-Publication Data

Swan, James.
    Fundraising for the small public library : a how-to-do-it manual for
librarians / by James Swan.
        p.   cm. — (How-to-do-it manuals for libraries ; no. 8)
    Includes bibliographical references (p.   ) and index.
    ISBN 1-55570-077-2
    1. Library fund raising.   2. Small libraries—Finance.   3. Public
libraries—Finance.   I. Title.   II. Series.
Z683.S83   1990
025.1′1—dc20   90-6457
                                                              CIP

This book is dedicated to the memory of Lucille M. Thorne, friend, mentor, and advocate. She gave me my first job in a library and encouraged me as a professional.

CONTENTS

PREFACE

Libraries everywhere need more money to do what only they do best—provide knowledge, information and reading materials to the public. Small libraries seem less able to weather the storms of a declining tax base, and the onslaught of property tax protests. Most are already existing on the edge of poverty, lacking the ability to absorb even the slightest downturn in the economy. This book is for all the people who work in small libraries and feel the need to go beyond allocations from the city or county and work for something better for their library.

If you need a burst of enthusiasm and more than a little encouragement about the money situation in your library, *Fundraising for the Small Public Library* is for you. You can do something to make things better for your library.

ACKNOWLEDGMENTS

I would like to thank Milo Nelson, former editor of *Wilson Library Bulletin* for encouraging me to expand an article on fundraising into a book. I would like to thank the librarians and trustees who responded to the surveys. They provided much of the primary source information used in the book. I would like to thank staff members and boards of the Central Kansas Library System and the Great Bend Public Library for enduring my "hibernation" during the final days of preparing the manuscript. I especially want to thank professional fundraising consultants Joan Flanagan, Jean Rahn, and Robert Hartsook for ideas presented in their workshops. Many thanks to Jane Rutledge, formerly with the Friends of the Lawrence (Kansas) Public Library, whose article in the Friends' newsletter *FoKL Point*, provided many of the good ideas in Chapter 13. And most of all, I would like to thank my family, who sensed my enthusiasm and understood my absence from the home and still encouraged me. And a special thanks to Diana. She helped me see the flaws in my thinking, and my typing.

Author's Note: Some of the donor names used in this book are made up to protect their privacy.

INTRODUCTION

Don't I know you? Haven't we met somewhere before?

I may not know you personally, but I know who you are, because you are reading this book. Aren't you the librarian of a small public library somewhere in suburban or rural America? Or perhaps you are the board chair. I know you because you have been in my workshops. Sometimes you were alone and felt that no one cared enough about your library to come with you. Sometimes you felt isolated because of the overwhelming task of running a library with half enough money and too little help. But still you kept on working because you believed in your library and what it could do for the community. You cared about it.

Today, you still care about your library, but you wish others would share your commitment. Right now, you are looking for ways to help bolster a sagging budget. You probably need a new library or just more space, and you don't know where to find the money to solve the problem. Maybe you are wishing for a genie to change things, or for the reincarnation of Andrew Carnegie. The truth is that you are willing to work hard, but every fundraising effort seems to involve a great deal of work for a disappointingly small gain.

Fundraising for the Small Public Library is not an Aladdin's lamp which, if rubbed three times, will give you three wishes and all the money you want. But if you have the determination to read it and the courage to try some of its suggestions, you will have the power to improve funding for your library. You *can* make a difference.

Kris Adams Wendt of the Rhinelander District Library in Wisconsin said, "If I had to select one truth to pass on to others it would be this: Stop sitting around at meetings wringing your hands at the enormity of your goal, wishing for the second coming of Andrew Carnegie and saying 'Now is not the right time to do something like this.' Get up, get out, and do something positive! Our million-dollar project began with children collecting 100 pennies to bring to the library."

Robert Hartsook, a fundraising executive for Wichita State University, Kansas, said, "Fundraising in libraries has explosive potential. It is an idea whose time has come. Libraries have a built-in constituent base and they provide a universally appealing service."

The best way to raise money for your library is to decide on a

1

project, determine how much it will cost, and ask people for the money to pay for it.

For me, library fundraising started the day I walked three blocks from the library to the bank in Easley, South Carolina. I was on my way to ask the bank president for $300 to pay for a library publicity booklet published by Channing-Bete, a company that publishes promotional brochures for libraries and other nonprofit organizations.

I recall that event in a flood of warm feelings. I didn't know much about fundraising then, so it must have been providence guiding me. But more than likely it was dumb luck. Somehow, though, I did something right because I walked out of the bank with $300.

Since then, I have been learning and sharing what I have learned with other librarians and trustees. I have attended hundreds of workshops and seminars. I put the principles and techniques I learned into practice in my own library. Then I started teaching others. I have given over 150 workshops on public library management. Topics have included fundraising, budgeting, group decision-making, brainstorming, planning, etc. Along the way I have picked up thousands of ideas from hardworking, caring librarians just like you.

A Workshop

Think of this book as a workshop. As you read, imagine that your board has sent you away to a two-day workshop on fundraising for small public libraries. This workshop is filled with handouts, checklists, forms and successful fundraising ideas that have worked for libraries just like yours. Jot down impressions as they come to you, just as you would in a workshop. When you finish, you will return to your library with enthusiasm and many action ideas you will want to try right away. You don't even have to finish the book to try an idea. You could do something today to bring money to your library.

Maybe you will be like the librarian who had on her on her to-do list, "Contact Mr. Conrad for a donation to the library's building fund." Conrad was the owner of a large department store. She was in the store one day on personal business when the thought came to her, "Go see Mr. Conrad *now*." But, "No," she thought, "I'm not dressed for it. I'm not ready." The idea persisted: "Do it now." Still she resisted: "He is probably not in. Maybe he is too busy. He won't see me." But, despite her misgivings, she mustered her courage, found her way to the office receptionist, and asked to see Mr. Conrad. He was in. He graciously invited her into his office and listened to her brief presentation. She had practiced it a hundred times in her mind. Now she was giving it in person. She boldly asked him for $3,000, hoping for $1,000. She walked out of the store with $2,000 for the library.

Listen to the thoughts that come to you as you read this book. *Act on them right away.* They are valuable inspirations.

Begin by asking yourself some fundamental questions: Are you the only one in your library who feels the way you do about fundraising? Do you feel all alone? Is there no one else to share your enthusiasm?

What can you do to gain some support? Think for a minute. Is there one person on your board who shares your concern about library funding?

There is?

Excellent!

When you find an idea that grabs you, share it with that friend. Share this book with your ally. Then the two of you can develop a plan to involve others.

Are you already involved in fundraising?

You are? Great!

You will probably encounter some ideas you have already tried, and some you haven't. Maybe you will turn up a new twist on an old idea. Or perhaps you will give your own twist to a concept you find in the book. The purpose of this book is to expand your thinking on the potential of fundraising.

What a blessing it would have been to have had a "how-to-do-it" book on fundraising for the small public library *before* I walked into that bank in South Carolina. It could have saved me agonizing over how to approach a potential donor, or how to plan a fundraising activity using community resources and talent.

My effort was successful because I followed these simple rules for fundraising:

1. Have a specific donor in mind. *The bank.*
2. Have a specific project in mind. *The booklet.*
3. Give the donor something—a benefit or a good feeling. *The bank's name on the back of the booklet.*
4. Help the donor visualize the product. *A sample copy of the booklet with a pasteup of the custom printed page.*
5. Have a specific amount in mind. *$300.* (I was confi-

dent that the amount was within the bank's giving capacity.)
6. Ask for the gift expecting to receive it.

Although libraries everywhere are involved in exciting, successful fundraising activities, too many are not. Over one-third of the librarians I surveyed indicated that their libraries were not involved in fundraising. What a pity! They could be tapping into a pipeline of generosity for their library.

You may not be connected with a library. You may be a scout leader or the president of the PTA. That's all right! Most of the material in this book can be used by any nonprofit organization. Many ideas found here come from nonlibrary settings. The thrust of this book is to help organizations in small communities meet their financial needs through fundraising. Whether you are working with Girl Scouts, Boy Scouts, 4-H, or the high school band, you can find something here to put to work in your group next week. The planning forms and checklists will be just as valuable to you as they are to a librarian. The principles in this book apply to all community groups.

Are you ready?

If you can't take a corporate president to lunch and ask for $50,000 or $100,000, read on. This book is for fundraisers who must rely on community resources rather than on large corporations or foundations.

Are you ready for a fundraising project?

You are not sure?

If you are not sure, you are probably not ready!

Complete the Fundraising Readiness Checklist to see how ready you really are. If you have trouble answering any of these questions, we have helped you isolate some inherent shaky spots in your fundraising effort. You are on your way toward overcoming these weaknesses.

Fundraising Readiness Checklist

1. ORGANIZATIONAL READINESS
• Do you have a brief statement describing the mission of your library?

- Is your library succeeding at its mission?
- Do you have a one-page description of the project you would like to accomplish?
- Can you list the benefits of the project?
- Does your library have strong internal leadership?
- Does the public perceive your library as a relevant, successful, and a meaningful part of the community?

2. MARKET RESEARCH

- Who will give to your cause?
  Make a list right now of five people you can ask for a donation of $100.

- Who cares about your service?
  Make a list of five people who care about the library.

- What groups benefit from your services?
  Make a list of five groups who care about the library.

3. HUMAN RESOURCES

- Are staff members knowledgeable and effective fundraisers?
- Are board members well-known, well-respected individuals in the area you serve?
- Are board members willing to become involved in fundraising?
- Are they willing to contribute to the cause?
- Do you have a committed group of volunteers who will provide prospects and ask those prospects for money?
- Will these volunteers make a gift themselves?

4. FUNDRAISING VEHICLES.
How will you raise the money?

Direct mail
Phone-a-thons
Special events
Personal solicitation campaigns
Memorials
Direct mail campaign
Foundations grants
Corporate grants
Auctions
Book sales
Bequests
Life insurance policies
Trusts
Capital campaign

If you felt vague about your answers to any of these questions, you may have identified a restraining force. Before you can be successful you will have to deal with its hampering effect.

MARKETING IS THE KEY

"The best books on fundraising haven't been written. Most books on fundraising don't include marketing" says Thomas S. Parish, coordinator of external funding and professor of human development with the College of Education at Kansas State University. Parish, a master salesman himself, is a top fundraiser for the College of Education at KSU. He once called 187 former students of the College of Education and secured donations from 183.

Most books on fundraising focus on the success of others—telling how someone else succeeded in another setting and another time. While *Fundraising for the Small Public Library* spotlights fundraising successes of various small libraries, it is unique because it teaches you how to think creatively. It gives you the tools to take a idea—yours or someone else's—and make it work for you.

A community based approach

The basis of successful fundraising is the community—your community. An idea that worked in Woodstock, New York, might not work in Live Oak, Florida, where Danny Hales is the librarian. A Woodstock idea can work if Danny takes it and gives it a Florida twist and his own brand of enthusiasm. He knows how to mold and reshape things to fit the thinking of his community. Danny knows his community. He knows how to make things happen in Live Oak, Florida.

You know how to make things happen in your community. Every checklist, planning form, and concept in this book is designed to be changed by you. Every thought is meant to be a springboard to an idea for you to reshape and use in your community. Brainstorming and planning are the group processes that will turn someone else's notion into a practical project in your community.

Challenge these ideas

You may challenge some of the opinions expressed here. I hope you do. I don't claim to know all the answers, and I most assuredly don't know the fundraising answers for your community. I know what has worked for some libraries and why. What worked for them may not work for you. My biases may show through. For example, I don't like gambling in any form as a means of raising money for the library. I think it sends the wrong message to library patrons. But if raffles, bingo, or casino night are the norm in your community, go ahead and try them. If they worked for others in your town, they will probably work for you, too.

I will try to warn you away from fundraising events that don't work very well for anyone. Special events are activities that generally don't work as fundraisers. They are great for having a good time or raising the library's visibility, but not worth the effort when it comes to making money.

The library in Claflin, Kansas (population 600) had a polka party and made about $300. They would have lost money on the event if the dance hall hadn't been free and if the band hadn't discounted its fee by $150. As it turned out, everyone had a good time, but the library doesn't plan to do it again.

Use an action plan

At most of my workshops I ask people to write an action plan by writing down three ideas they plan to implement when they return to their libraries. On page 9 is an action plan form. Make a copy of it right now and as you get ideas you want to try, jot them down. Then try them as soon as you can.

When you find three ideas and put them to work, you will have paid for the book and I will be pleased.

Action Plan

Fundraising Idea.	How can I change the idea to make it work in our community?	When will I do it?

1 SMALL LIBRARIES, BIG GOALS

The library in Jewell, Kansas, has about 200 square feet inside, including storage and a rest room. Every time the librarian, Ava Kelly, buys a new book she has to take another one off the shelf—and she knows every book in the library. Her patrons send their children to the library with a note that says, "You know what I like to read. Please send me three or four books you think I will like." Talk about customer service! You can't do that in a large library. Patron support has to be high. If a library like Jewell does a good job at giving the people what they want, it will always have the public support it needs, even when the economy is bad.

This is the key to raising money for small public libraries. Give people what they want when they come to the library, and they will make sure the library has the funding it needs. If tax support isn't enough, they will go out and raise the money some other way. A client-centered approach is the only way to guarantee adequate funding for the library.

Small libraries can be bright cheerful places where families can feel at home. Places where the librarian can visit with you about the books on the shelf because she has read most of them. The librarian can sit at a regular desk and visit with the people as they come in. In fact, my favorite small libraries have nice, soft chairs next to the librarian's desk. Small public libraries are warm, comfortable people places. Why is it, then, that small public libraries are finding an increasing need to conduct fundraising projects?

Here are some observations about libraries in small towns:

- Small towns are primarily in rural parts of the country.
- Populations are declining in small towns in rural America.
- On average, their populations are older.
- Property values are declining.
- Per capita support for small libraries (in Kansas) is about 25 percent less than it is for larger libraries.
- Libraries in communities of 300 need as much space as libraries in communities of 2,000.
- In central Kansas it costs as much to provide library service to 200 people as to 800 people, and it costs almost as much to provide library service to 1,000 people as to 3,000 people.

The basic problem for all small public libraries is they lack the resources available to large public libraries. They cannot take advantage of the economies of scale. The adage "It takes money to make money" applies to fundraising, too. Unfortunately, the resources needed for "seed money" to raise extra cash are not available to many small public libraries; they can barely keep the

WHAT IS A SMALL LIBRARY?

What is your assessment of a small library? Answer these questions and make your own determination:

What is the population of your town?

What do you consider large?

What are the advantages of living in a small town?

What are the disadvantages of living in a small town?

What are the advantages of living in a town you consider large?

What are the disadvantages?

What are the advantages to having a library in a small town?

What are the disadvantages?

If our library were in a large town or city we would be able to. . . .

If our library were in a large town or city, we would be forced to deal with. . .

The things I like best about a small town library are. . . .

If you can answer these questions candidly, you can discover new ways of thinking about being small and how you can benefit from it. All of the fundraising ideas in this book have been used by people in small libraries. When you see a good idea you want to try, put it to work immediately.

library open. When limited resources are used to raise money, it takes a proportionately larger share to raise a lesser amount; for example, you cannot expect to raise $150,000 for $15,000 if it costs $50,000 to raise $500,000. It will probably cost nearer $20,000 to raise $150,000. Fundraising costs will vary according to the activity, the project, and the community.

Small is relative

There seems to be no universally accepted standard to define a small public library. Some have suggested a population of 25,000, and for the purposes of this book I have used that figure. In Kansas, 298 of the 311 public libraries serve populations of less than 25,000. In other states the percentage may not be as high.

When I say small town, I mean towns like McCracken, Kansas, where the population of 292 is declining every month. The library has an operating budget of just over $3,000. That isn't even enough to keep the library open for ten hours a week and pay a librarian the minimum wage, let alone have enough money to pay the heat and light bill and buy a few books. Not only is the library small, but it's also isolated. The nearest other library is 18 miles away. So many libraries are just like McCracken. Fundraising is their key to survival.

Even the smallest of small libraries needs $10,000 a year to operate. Fundraising is the only way they can afford to be open at least 15 hours per week, have a collection of at least 6,000 current titles, subscribe to 30 magazines, and be housed in a building of at least 2,000 square feet. Below these minimums, a tiny library is more like a reading room than a library. But if they have the support of a good library system and an active fundraising effort, they can survive—and even thrive.

Advantages of being small

Being small has its advantages. Small libraries tend to be closer to their communities, and as such they can win public support in a big way. The Rhinelander (Wisconsin) District library raised $250,000 to remodel a Carnegie Library. They involved the community in a way that gave the people a sense of ownership. Citizens participated on the project from the beginning and were much prouder of the resulting facility than if they had actually found a mythical "Carnegie-esque" philanthropist.

Librarian Kris Adams Wendt said they broke their fundraising project down into terms an average library supporter could do something about: "I can't raise a million dollars by myself, but I can bake a pie, hold a car wash, set up a lemonade stand, belly dance at birthday parties, dress a doll for an auction, etc."

The sense of community is strong in small-town America. Small-town people are committed to their community. They are physically and emotionally close to their library. They are part of it and it belongs to them.

The people in Ellis, Kansas (population 2,500) raised over $260,000 in private donations for a new library—a per capita level to be envied by any fundraising group. Volunteers personally asked everyone in town to make a donation to the library building fund.

You can make your own list of things that make small libraries special. Think about your own library and your largest neighbor. What are the things about your library that make a difference? Write down your library's good points. How can you turn them into assets for fundraising?

As a graduate student a Clarion State University, Timothy Lynch conducted a survey of trustees in small libraries. He found that trustees from small libraries were more likely to become involved in the administration of the library. How could you turn a trend like that into an asset? Do you know everyone in town? Do they love the library? Do they go to church? Do they have a habit of giving to their church? Can you turn this trait into dollars for your library?

People in small towns are older than the general population, and older people tend to give more money to charity than their younger neighbors. How can you capitalize on this combination?

Overcoming Limitations

Libraries fortunate enough to afford the services of a professional librarian are blessed indeed. Diane Gordon Kadanoff, director of the Norwell Public Library, Massachusetts says, "While small may imply limitations imposed on the library by itself, it does not necessarily mean limitations on the skill, talents, creativity of the professional staff. They learn to do everything with a degree of expertise. . ." ("Small Libraries—No Small Job!," *Library Journal,* March 1, 1986, p. 72-73)

Indeed, that is what I discovered when I found myself fresh out of library school, and running a county library in South Carolina. I became everything from a circulation clerk to a reference librarian to a budget presenter at county council meetings. The next day I was back in the library installing light tubes or mowing the lawn. I became a public relations expert, a fundraiser, and a storyteller. But the best thing about being in a small library is the opportunity to try lots and lots of ideas. Somehow it was easier to fail on a small scale and survive. Some of my projects might have been failures, but I learned from every one.

Joan Flanagan, fundraising consultant and author of *The Grass Roots Fundraising Book,* says, "The best answers are the ones you develop in your own area. It doesn't matter how small you are. You can raise as much money as you want in your own area."

You can also take the list of observations about small towns and look for the silver linings. When you develop the skill of turning a presumed disadvantage into an advantage, you will have unlocked the door to successful fundraising in small public libraries. Here is the list. Try to find at least three advantages for each:

ADVANTAGES OF SMALL TOWN LIBRARIES

Think of as many advantages as you can for each of the following observations:

Small libraries are in small towns.

Small towns are primarily in rural parts of the country.

Populations are declining in small towns in rural America.

Populations are older in small towns in rural America.

Property values are declining in rural small towns.

Per capita support for small libraries is about 25 percent less than it is for larger libraries.

Libraries in communities of 300 need as much space as libraries in communities of 2,000.

All small public libraries, regardless of the size of the community served, need 6,000 books.

THE BEST IN YOUR COMMUNITY

The best thing your community has going for its library right now is you!

Believe it!

You are not small minded. Your goals are not small.

You have just been appointed to take charge! Go ahead!

One of the worst things fundraisers do is to set their goals too low. You will not make that mistake. You are learning how to think big and raise the money you need for your project. One of Murphy's Laws is "Everything costs more than it costs." It means you will have to raise more money than you think if you are going to have the computer you want or the new library with all the furniture you need.

Do you have a project in mind right now? What do you want to do? Come on! Every good library leader has a wish list. Write it down. How much do you think it will cost? Write the amount down. Now add ten percent. That should give you a realistic fundraising goal.

You are the one who will motivate others. You know you need a new building. You can sell the idea to at least two other people. They can sell it to five others, and so on. If you don't start it, who will? You are the one reading this book. You are the one who is gathering all the ideas. All you have to do is communicate your ideas to others. Why not call up a friend right now and share an idea you have already learned from this book. Ask him or her if it will work in your town. Are they willing to help you give it try? Why not? Ask, "How can we work together to make it happen?"

Who is going to motivate others? You are!

You have to be convinced of the need.

You have to convince others of the need.

OVERCOMING NEGATIVE FORCES

Negative forces are those elements in your community that will keep you from getting what you need to give people what they want when they come to the library. You can make your own list. I'll give you a start.

- A negative force is a city council whose members don't read or use the library.
- A negative force is a slow economy or a shift in political power.
- A negative force is a powerful politician or a closed-minded bureaucrat who doesn't appreciate libraries.
- A negative force is unruly children in the library.
- A negative force is a librarian who is so stern and unfriendly that people won't come back to the library.
- A negative force is a stagnating board with individuals who have been sitting so long their brains won't function.

Anything that keeps you from doing a good job for your patrons can be a negative force.

My doctor in South Carolina once asked the president of the county council why he didn't give the library more money. His answer was: "I would like to, but three of the five councilmen can't read." What a negative force to overcome! I am not sure I ever did. Sometimes we have to wait for a better political climate. It's like letting the accumulated trash in the water hose clear out so it won't clog the sprinkler. You have to wait for time to cleanse the system.

Negative forces sometimes help us clean up our act. I am aware of libraries that had "baby sitters of books" for librarians. Things got so bad that the board finally took action and brought in a new librarian. Circulation doubled. People who hadn't been to the library for years returned. Mayors have been won over because a librarian perceived them as a negative force and began to pay attention to their needs. When the mayor got what he wanted, the library got what it needed. A real win-win situation.

Seeing ourselves as others see us

Sometimes a negative force can help us see ourselves as others see us. When was the last time you walked around the block and came into your library through the front door? Did you count the 11 steep steps to the front door? Were you puffing by the time you got to the top? When you opened the door, what was your first impression? Was everything so closed and forbidding that you felt like turning around and walking out or, better yet, running out? Or were you greeted by an open, airy feeling—one that drew you into the library and made you feel welcome? Did you feel the way you want others to feel when they come into your library?

What did you discover? Is there a list of prohibitives on the front door? "No food, drink, or smoking." Or, "We cannot check out a book without a library card." Were there so many displays that you could barely wiggle your way past them into the library? Was there enough parking outside the library? What psychological barriers did you see that kept people from using the library? Was the person at the circulation desk frowning and unfriendly?

Is the physical appearance of your library a negative force?

If it is, stop right now!

Make a list of five things you could do next week to make your library more inviting and attractive. You can make a difference in the way others perceive your library.

Motiving your board

If you have an appointed board that doesn't want to ask others for money, you need help. First of all you have to understand their position. It is not wrong for them to think that they did not "hire on" as fundraisers. And they aren't about to start now. Every time you try to make changes that will cost money, they drag their feet. You need some help. The board is the recognized authority for the library. They have the power. But where do you go?

Here are some suggestions:

- Try working with the Friends of the Library. If you don't have a Friends group, organize one. We need all the friends we can get. There is detailed information on how to go about this in Chapter 14.
- With the board's approval, organize a fundraising steering committee or a special projects committee.

- Get the help of a single board member and develop a plan to involve the rest of the board.

BRAINSTORMING

The key to a successful fundraising effort in your community may be your ability to brainstorm. You sit down with a group of people who have the library's interest in common and think creatively. Brainstorming is a marvelous technique that can produce exciting, often unexpected results. You start with a group of seven to ten people who are somewhat familiar with the problem. It is not necessary that everyone know everything about the operation of the library. Sometimes it is better if they don't. Set aside one hour of uninterrupted time. Assign two or more people to be note takers—one primary note taker and a couple of "reserves," in case the flow of ideas gets too fast for one person to record it all. (Some brainstorming facilitators I know like to use large sheets of paper on an easel or taped to the wall.) Select a leader whose job it is to direct the discussion. Select someone else to do the writing. The facilitator encourages participation by making positive statements about the process. For example: "We are going great. Let's keep it up. What else can we think of?" The leader reminds everyone of the rules if that becomes necessary.

RULES FOR BRAINSTORMING

1. Appoint a time keeper and set a time limit: Twenty minutes is usually an optimum amount for the creative phase of brainstorming.

2. Encourage everyone to contribute: You can start by going around the table. If a person can't think of anything the first time around, move on to the next person. Maybe he or she will the next time. Soon everyone will respond spontaneously.

3. Write down all ideas as they are given: The leader may repeat what has been said to give the contributor a chance to clarify the idea.

4. Make no evaluation of any kind during the process: Negative comments are especially discouraged, including negative body language or laughing at an idea.

Brainstorming works best when the group focuses on a specific question: "How can we raise $5,000 in the next six months in order to buy new carpet for the library." Write your focusing question on a blackboard or separate chart where everyone can see it.

Once people loosen up and get into the process, the ideas will flow. A group of seven secretaries once came up with 256 ideas in one 20-minute brainstorming session. It took five of them to write down all of the ideas. They weren't hampered by restraining thoughts of what wouldn't work or fearfulness of offending a supervisor. Not all of the ideas were used, but think of the power this method has for creating solutions.

You can practice brainstorming on your own. Start by clearing your mind and your work space of all distractions. Get rid of the visual noise. Write your focusing question on the first sheet of a pad of paper: "How can I put together a fundraising group by July 1st." Then quietly relax and let thoughts come to you. Write them down as they come.

The following is an example of individual brainstorming. We wanted to help many of our small libraries buy a telefacsimile machine. I came up with these fundraising ideas in about 20 minutes.

FUNDRAISING IDEAS FOR YOUR FAX MACHINE
If you think you would like to have a FAX machine, but can't afford one, here are a few suggestions that might help.

Solicit donations: Point out the benefit of having a FAX machine at the library. Tell how it will help them in their business and ask for a $25 donation. Offer to send their first FAX message free.

Take on a partner: Possibilities include the city, the school, the county extension office, a lawyer, an insurance agent or other business professional, a bank.

Share the cost of operation: You pay for the supplies and maintenance: your partner pays for the monthly telephone charges.

Take on several partners: Let one pay for the maintenance, another for the telephone charges, and another the supplies.

Sell coupons for future use: Rather than just asking businesses in town to help pay for the FAX machine, offer them coupons (at a discount) good for sending FAX messages whenever they need to.

Pay for ongoing costs by charging: Charge $5 to send the first five pages and $1 a page thereafter.

Put a donation can in the library: Label it with the message: "Help us get a FAX machine." Point out the benefits to them such as: quicker response to interlibrary loan requests; opportunity for the community to send urgent messages out via FAX.

Name the FAX machine contest: Have children submit names for the FAX machine, then have the public vote by putting quarters in different jars.

The next phase of brainstorming is to clarify and combine ideas. If two ideas are similar, the contributors may clarify them into one suggestion, building on differences. If some ideas are not clear, the leader asks for clarification from the person who made them. The exciting part of this phase is the creative twists the group gives to the ideas. Someone might have suggested putting a flyer out asking people to give money for the carpet. Someone else suggests putting the flyer in the books patrons check out.

Brainstorming sessions are synergistic activities designed to create ideas that build on each other. The whole becomes greater than the sum of its parts.

In a brainstorming session of a library fundraising group in Ellsworth, Kansas, someone suggested writing a letter to Santa Claus. Maybe the situation seemed so hopeless that a letter to Santa seemed as good an idea as any. After the expected round of smiles and laughs, the note taker wrote down the idea and the group moved on.

In the next phase of the process—clarifying and combining—someone suggested that they go ahead and write a letter to Santa Claus and publish it in the local newspaper. They did, listing several items the library needed. The bank bought a $600 set of encyclopedias. Others gave money. The net proceeds from a letter to Santa was $2,500. The next year a similar letter yielded $3,000. The library's letter to Santa Claus has become an annual event.

What would have happened if someone had said, "What a stupid idea. It will never work"? Two outcomes are possible—both of them bad. The person who made the suggestion might not have made another suggestion, and the library would have missed out on a "golden goose" fundraising idea.

Brainstorming Exercise

WHAT COULD YOU DO WITH . . .

From the list of materials listed below, develop with your group a strategy for raising $1,000. You may use you imagination to fill in the details of size, color, quality, etc. Develop as many projects as you can in 20 minutes. Spend the first ten minutes working individually, then share ideas among the group for about ten minutes—longer if you are on a roll. You may use some items more than once, if you use them on different projects. You may assume that members of the group have the necessary tools or utensils to produce the products you decide on.

1,000 sheets of paper

1,000 envelopes

1 roll of contact paper

4 pairs of scissors

1 bag of flour

1 bag of sugar

1 bag of pinto beans

1 container of cinnamon

1 bag of yeast

1 set of felt tip markers

1 container of paint

1 bag of nails

200 board feet of lumber

$100 in cash.

The third phase of brainstorming is evaluating and implementing the ideas. This can occur at the original meeting of the group if you are in a hurry, but it is usually better to let the ideas percolate for about a week. When the group reconvenes, they review all of the ideas and clarify them again. Perhaps someone has another twist. By now the sense of ownership of ideas is distanced by time, and people are not as sensitive to critical comments about their suggestions.

You will be surprised at the power of allowing the subconscious mind to work on the problem. In the time between the idea generation session and the evaluation and implementation session, new thoughts will come to you and variations on other suggestions will enhance the process.

Review the original focus question. Then ask, "Which of all these ideas seem to have the best chance of success at achieving our goal?" A way to avoid direct confrontation is to ask the group to vote on their favorite three or four ideas—ranking them—1-2-3 in order of preference. The one that gets the most votes becomes the project for the group.

On this page and the next are two brainstorming exercises for fundraising groups designed to get you thinking about converting available resources into marketable products. Copy them and use them as a worksheet with your group.

Brainstorming is the best opportunity you will have to create enthusiasm among your group members. You will hear exclamations like, "That's a great idea! Let's go for it!" "I can get Bill Smith to donate the paint." It is the beginning of converting ideas into action. Never underestimate the excitement brainstorming can generate.

Team building and commitment

This is where the seeds of commitment are planted and begin to grow. Individuals develop a sense of ownership—even if the idea selected for the project didn't come from them. The team came up with a great idea, and they are a member of the team. Don't bypass brainstorming even if you have a hundred great, proven, and tried ideas. Not only does brainstorming lead to some great ideas, it also generates a team spirit and promotes group cohesiveness.

Are you looking for zippy new fundraising ideas that make people say, "What a great idea! Why didn't I think of that?" Why not bring together a bunch of different people who don't know each other? Ask them to brainstorm. New groups are especially

Brainstorming Exercise

DISCOVERING AND USING COMMUNITY RESOURCES

This worksheet helps a fundraising group focus on resources available in the community. It takes the group from a contrived situation to a real one. You can use this outline to develop fundraising strategies based on local resources. Make photocopies and use it with your group. Go around the group and let each person respond to each question. Have someone write the responses in the space after each question.

1. What products does our community produce that are unique?

2. What skills do individuals have that can be used for the good of the community?

3. What do members of our community like to do? (work or recreation)

4. How can we turn this interest into a fundraiser?

5. What events have attracted people from outside the community?

6. How can we piggyback on one of these events and make money?

7. Is there a community need that can be filled in a way that will make money?

responsive to brainstorming. They may lack a sense of connection with your library, but their ideas will be fresh. Some of the most creative ideas and most enthusiastic responses come from newly formed groups.

The most important thing to remember about brainstorming is, "Don't allow negative comments in the creative process." Regardless of how strange it may sound, don't criticize, reject or laugh at any idea.

SURVEY OF TRUSTEES

The way library board members perceive their roles can be a problem for fundraisers. In 1989 I sent a four-page survey to 350 library trustees in the Central Kansas Library System. The System has 54 library boards with seven appointed members on each board. Populations represented range from 42,000 to 110, with a mean of 670. More than half of the libraries are in towns of less than 1,000 people. Here are some of the major conclusions:

- The smaller the library, the more willing trustees are to become involved in its day-to-day operations.
- The smaller the library, the more willing trustees are to give instructions to staff members.
- The smaller the library, the more willing trustees are to have a high profile in the management of the library.
- Trustees of larger libraries tend to have more formal education than trustees of smaller libraries.
- Trustees of smaller libraries tend to be older than trustees of larger libraries.
- Trustee of smaller libraries tend to have more frequent contacts with the librarians than trustees of larger libraries.

Two major fundraising conclusions from the survey were:

- Ninety-three percent did not believe that fundraising was a basic responsibility of the library board of trustees.
- The smaller the library, the less willing trustees were to give even a modest gift of $25 to a major fundraising campaign.

One question posed by the survey was, "If your library had to raise money equal to ten times your budget for a new building or other project, what would be your most difficult task? In order of frequency, the most common responses were:

1. convincing the community and themselves of the need;
2. concern over the depressed economy in the area;
3. gaining community support;
4. soliciting in the community;
5. finding the right project;
6. recruiting volunteers;
7. planning and organizing the project;
8. finding the right leadership;
9. obtaining support from city officials for increasing taxes.

Nearly 30 percent of the respondents did not answer the question—most likely because they didn't want to grapple with the problem. Since many respondents from larger libraries already have adequate libraries, it was difficult for them to see the question as a real problem. Respondents in the smallest libraries, however, could identify with the question. Nevertheless, it is a problem most public library trustees are not anxious to face.

More than likely, your board faces some of the same concerns. Some members might have responded differently, but these responses seem to be typical among trustees in small libraries across the country. (The complete survey is at the end of this chapter, in case you would like to replicate it in your own area.)

Trustees are struggling with the main charge of being a trustee—balancing their concern for adequate library service and the demands on the community to pay for it. In small libraries the struggle seems more intense. The lack of responses to the question on fundraising spotlights the immobilizing effect that problem can have. If it isn't the library board's job to raise money for the library, whose job is it? You have to be the catalyst for change.

NATIONAL SURVEY

Because most of my anecdotal information for this book came from experiences in South Carolina and Kansas, and because I wanted to share fundraising experiences of librarians from around the country, I conducted a national survey of librarians and their fundraising activities. I contacted 75 libraries in communities of less than 25,000 in ten states. I asked them the following questions about their fundraising activities:

- What was the purpose of your fundraising project?
- What did you do? Briefly describe the project.
- What was the source of the idea for the fundraising activity?
- Who did most of the work?
- What went well? (Or what was the major problem, if you are describing a failure.)
- If people in another library wanted to use this idea to raise money, what would you suggest they do differently?
- What was the community response to your fundraiser?
- Did something unexpected happen?
- How much money did this project raise?
- Was it worth it?

Librarians responded with anecdotal material illustrating many of the points of this book. Here is a general summary of their responses:

The most common fundraising purpose was to remodel an existing building or build a new one. Several libraries raised money for new carpeting or a photocopier or computer. Most projects involved selling a service or product, but the ones that raised the most money involved organized solicitation. Friends of the library were often listed as those in charge of the project. The librarian and a few volunteers also were next on the list of those who did most of the work. Community involvement was the most often mentioned key to success. Suggestions for improving the process were all over the map; more and better trained volunteers seemed to head the list. Community response, almost without exception, was reported as very positive—supporting the idea that fundraising for small public libraries is an idea whose time has come. The answer to whether it was it worth it was split. Several of those who responded, especially those who produced something and sold it, felt that the work was disproportionately hard for the money they made. Those who solicited money were pleased with the result of their effort, even though it was a lot of work. The most frequent suggestion was, "Recruit more volunteers. Don't try to do all the work yourself."

Learn from others

Yogi Berra says, "You can see a lot just by observing." Learn to observe the fundraising techniques of other groups; you can learn a lot from them. Don't throw away those fundraising letters you get in the mail every day. Keep them. Study them and figure out how to put your own twist to an idea you see. Become an expert observer. Then put that expertise to work for your library by reshaping the idea to make it work for you.

SUMMARY

Your success as a fundraiser will come from your ability to assess the strengths of individuals in your community and mobilize them into a cohesive support for the library. As you analyze your community and its needs and the library and its needs, you will discover that your success will come in proportion to how well the two needs are matched. Your job as a fundraiser is to convince your donor that it is in his or her best interest to contribute to your project. How to do it is what the rest of *Fundraising for the Small Public Library* is about.

LIBRARY BOARD QUESTIONNAIRE

❑ Board President   ❑ Board Member

1.   Please indicate whether you **A**gree, **D**isagree or are **N**eutral about the following statements.

A   D   N   a.)   The library board should maintain a low profile in the day to day management of the library.

A   D   N   b.)   The librarian should not purchase controversial materials without first consulting the library board.

A   D   N   c.)   The job of the librarian is first and foremost to suggest books for the patron to read.

A   D   N   d.)   A masters degree in library science is a necessary requirement for one to be a librarian.

A   D   N   e.)   The library board should be the sole group that determines the policies of the local library.

A   D   N   f.)   I don't think the people in the state library really care what is going on in our library.

A   D   N   g.)   I would not hesitate to give instructions to a library staff member if I saw something that needed to be done.

A   D   N   h.)   The basic responsibility of the library board is fundraising.

A   D   N   i.)   The library board is responsible for everything that happens in the library.

A   D   N   j.)   The library board knows what the community wants in terms of library service.

A   D   N   k.)   The library board does not know as much about libraries in general as the librarian.

A   D   N   l.)   The library board does not know as much about our library as the librarian.

A   D   N   m.)   The library is not the most important institution in the community.

A   D   N   n.)   Serving on the library board is a prestigious position.

A   D   N   o.)   It is O.K. for the librarian to do the bookkeeping for the library as part of his/her regular duties.

A   D   N   p.)   If the librarian were ill and if time would permit, I would feel comfortable to fill in for him/her.

A   D   N   q.)   If our library were conducting a major fundraising campaign, I would give $25.00 or more.

_____2. How many times per month do you have informal contact with the librarian outside of the library?

_____3. How often per month are you consulted by the librarian concerning library matters outside of the regularly scheduled board meeting?

_____4. How often per month are you consulted by the president of the board concerning library matters outside of the regularly scheduled board meeting?

_____5. Excluding the regularly scheduled board meeting, how many hours per month do you spend on library matters?

Yes   No   6. Do you know all of the library staff members by name?

            7. Have you ever participated in any of the following activities?
Yes   No   a.   Writing a grant proposal for the library.
Yes   No   b.   Speaking on behalf of the library at club meetings, etc.
Yes   No   c.   Participating on a fundraising committee.

            8. Please indicate how often you used the library within the past two months on non-board matters.
                  _____Never (0)
                  _____1-2
                  _____3-4
                  _____5 or more times

            9. How often within the past year have you been consulted about a library matter that you feel the librarian could or should have handled by himself/herself?
                  _____Never (0)
                  _____1-2
                  _____3-4
                  _____5 or more times

Yes   No   10. Have you ever offered unsolicited advice to the librarian concerning the operation of the library outside of a board meeting?
            Number of times within the past year?

If yes: What was the nature of that advice?
                  _____circulation policies
                  _____staffing
                  _____selection of books
                  _____matters concerning the library building or grounds
                  _____other. Please specify.

            11. If your library had to raise money equal to ten times your budget for a new building or another big project, what would be your most difficult task?

12.   Please state three major responsibilities of a board member.

13.   Why do you think you were selected to serve on the board of trustees?

Yes   No   14. Are you a member of any library association including ALA or KLA?

15.   How satisfied are you with your participation on the library board?
_____Very satisfied
_____Somewhat satisfied
_____Neither satisfied nor dissatisfied
_____Somewhat dissatisfied
_____Very dissatisfied

16.   What percent of the community knows that you serve on the library board?

17.   How often within the past year has a member of the community approached you with library matters?
_____Never (0)
_____1-2
_____3-4
_____5 or more times

Yes   No   18.   Has a member of the staff, other than the library director, ever come to you with concerns about the operation of the library?

Yes   No   19.   Have you ever entertained the librarian in your home?

Yes   No   20.   Have you ever participated in any of the programs, such as book discussions, offered at the library?

Yes   No   21.   Have you ever attended any of the programs, such as book discussions, offered at the library?

22.   How often do you have contact with other library board members between meetings?
_____Never (0)
_____1-2
_____3-4
_____5 or more times

Yes   No   23.   Are you presently a member of any other board or committee within your community?

24.   How long have you lived in this community?

25. How long have you served on the board?

26. Please indicate the highest level of formal schooling that you completed.

Yes   No   27. Are you currently employed?
_____Full-time
_____Part-time
_____Farm wife
_____Homemaker

Yes   No   28. Are you now enrolled in or have you ever taken a formal course in library
education? If yes, please specify.

29. How many CKLS workshops have you attended since your appointment to the board?

2 BASICS OF FUNDRAISING

"Cheshire Puss," Alice began. "Would you tell me, please, which way I ought to go from here?"

"That depends a good deal on where you want to get to," said the cat.

"I don't much care where . . . " said Alice.

"Then it doesn't matter which way you go," said the cat.

Lewis Carroll, *Alice in Wonderland*

Every good effort starts with a need. You are reading this book because you need more information about fundraising. This chapter offers a basic overview of the topic before we get to specifics.

Fundraising, simply put, is asking someone to support your cause by making a gift to the organization. Constituents, those who believe in your cause, will donate money because they feel good about contributing to it. Sometimes we call money-making projects—selling something—fund-raising. The only reason we sell something to someone to raise money is to reach nonconstituents—people who may be inclined to buy something from us if they feel they are receiving a reasonable return for their money.

The biggest problem with fundraising is not the donor. Almost everyone gives something to charity. The prime problem is the askers. Generally, people are reluctant to ask others for money because they are afraid they might be turned down. Perhaps it has happened before, and the sting of rejection still lingers.

We are used to working for what we earn. We cringe to think that we might be begging when we are raising funds for our library. How can we help our fundraisers overcome this negative connotation? We would much rather sell something tangible than ask for a gift outright. Isn't it the truth? Now think of this: How many bake sales will it take in your community to raise $100,000? If you want to raise a lot of money, you will have to ask people to give it to you.

People who do fundraising have to learn that soliciting a gift is not begging. It is selling. Sometimes the product we sell is not a traditional one. The product may be a good feeling or the knowledge that our money has done good for someone. It might be owning a "piece of the rock."

So a solution to overcoming the fear of asking is to think of our product in a different light. Our donor is buying a new wing for the library. Our donor is buying another year of continued enjoyment of the library. Our donor is repaying the community for being so good to him.

We have to be so confident that our cause is worthy of everyone's generosity that we go out enthusiastically and get people to buy a piece of our dream. After all, we buy things to make us feel better. We can spend $25 taking our family to the movies, and that doesn't include popcorn and drinks. When the show is over, sometimes we feel better and sometimes we don't. We buy a new dress or suit because it makes us feel good to wear new clothes. How did you feel the last time you bought a new (to you) car? We buy things because we believe they will make us feel better about ourselves. Think of fundraising as building self-esteem—giving people a chance to feel good about themselves.

FUNDRAISING IS ASKING

If this book had to be condensed into four words, these would be the four:

ASK FOR THE GIFT!

Sales people refer to this as "the close." Ken, a car dealer friend of mine, tells a story which makes this point better than anything I have heard.

"I went out to see this farmer at eight o'clock in the morning. I knew he was going to buy the car. I pitched that car every way I knew how. We drove around the country in it. I let him drive it. I sold it from six positions. I bought him lunch. I knew he was going to buy the car. That's why I stayed with him. We must have walked around that car 100 times. I must have gone over every feature at least 25. We went for another ride. When it was time for supper, I bought him supper. We were both getting tired, but I wasn't going to give up.

"All talked out, I sat down, exasperated. After 14 hours of selling the car every way I knew, finally and for the first time I said, 'Why don't you buy the car?' He said, 'Okay,' and we signed the papers."

Everyone likes to be asked. It makes them feel important. You can do your best job of selling anything, but if you don't ask for it, you won't get the sale. In fundraising you have to ask for the gift.

FUNDRAISING IS SELLING

Fundraising is basically selling. It is selling a product or an idea or just a good feeling. It is selling an investment in your cause. The trick is packaging the product in a way that will make the other person want to buy.

Jim Keller is one of the best sales people I know. He has been selling office products and equipment for at least 20 years. He uses what he calls "conversational selling." He says, "You have it in your mind that you are selling, but you don't want your prospects to feel that they are being sold something. You want to convey the idea that you are working for them or with them to solve their problems. To do that, you have to understand exactly what the customer has in mind."

Jim says, "Five essentials must be in place before someone will buy something. Whether you are going to buy a soda pop or a car, every one of these has to be in place, but they are not in any order:

- *Is it the right product?* If a farmer is looking for a pickup, don't try to sell him a sports car.
- *Need for the product.* If the prospect is thirsty, don't try to sell her a car.
- *Price.* Is the price within the prospect's ability and willingness to pay?
- *Time.* Is this the right time?
- *Is it the right vendor?* People do business with you because they like doing business with you.

"When I am not making progress, I stop and analyze where I am in the sales cycle. I try to determine where I am in relation to each of these five points. By asking questions I try to find out which of the five I haven't met."

Every one of these points is just as critical in fundraising. In fundraising, the product can be elusive. On the surface, you are asking someone to buy a product or donate to your cause. You may be emphasizing the benefit of your library to the community, but your prospect may be more interested in a visible way to remember her husband who died last year. Your job is to discover her need and sell the continued memory of her husband. In fundraising, your product has to be many things to many people.

Robert Hartsook, a professional fundraising consultant and the fundraising executive for Wichita State University, said that people give for one of two reasons:

1. Investment. They want to invest in what you are selling. They believe that their contribution to the library building fund is an investment in the future of the town, the lives of children, the memory of their parents, etc. They value one or more of the following:

- personal spirituality
- humanity
- personal gratitude
- perpetuation of ideas
- personal pride
- assurance of organizational goals.

2. Fear. Although they are concerned about your organization, they believe they won't see a return on their investment. Especially if you say, "We're going to have to close our doors if you don't give us something." Very few people will give because of fear. They may give if they feel strongly about:

- preventing want
- assuring the continuation of service.

Evaluating the prospect

Your research will help you evaluate the prospect. You have to evaluate his or her capacity to give, and interest in your organization. Objections to price usually hinge on one of these two things. Does the prospect have the cash to give to you? And does he or she want to give it to you?

Timing is a flexible variable, too. It may be the wrong time of the day, month, or year for your prospect. The best time for some people is right after payday. For others, it might be just before the end of the year. The prospect's tax preparer may be suggesting a charitable contribution to reduce tax liability. The easiest way to overcome a timing objection is to ask your donor, "When would be a better time." You may want to use a close associate of the prospect to discover the best time to make the contact. If he or she says, "Never," then timing is not the problem.

Jim Keller believes that people do business with him because they like doing business with *him*. Never underestimate the value of sending the right person to ask the right person for a gift—especially if you are looking for big donations. Often the who is more important than the how. The people you will involve in your project could make or break it. Choose them carefully—very carefully!

PRINCIPLES OF FUNDRAISING

While asking (selling) may be the most important step to fundraising, it is not the totality of the process. If it were, we wouldn't need books on the subject. Fundraisers have developed some techniques to help us organize our efforts and refine our methods so that we can raise more money with less effort and be successful more often.

Let's start with five principles that are essential to any successful fundraising effort.

1. Know how much you need and the purpose of your project. If you don't know the total cost of your project or why you need the money, your commitment will be weak. You don't have to share your goal with the donor, but you need to keep it clearly in mind.

2. Give before you ask. Everyone who asks others for money must give to their cause themselves. They must give enough to make a difference in the cause or in their own lives.

3. Ask for the gift. If you don't ask, you won't get (at least most of the time). Some libraries have been known to receive large gifts from unknown or unexpected sources. Don't count on it!

4. Ask the right person for the right amount. You don't pick one-pound tomatoes from a cherry tomato plant. You have to do your research if you want to know who to ask for a big gift.

5. Say thank you. Say thank you as many ways as you can. And recognize everyone who helped. Someone has said that you have to say thank you seven times before you can ask for another gift.

GIVE BEFORE YOU ASK

If you don't, you won't be convincing. Psychologists have discovered that people who ask others for donations without having given something themselves are less effective than those who have given. People who have given can say, "I gave to the project. Now it is your turn." They are confident and committed. If your prospects don't feel that you are convinced to the point of giving, they won't give either.

You might ask, "How much should I give?" The answer is up to you. But if you don't give what amounts to a sacrifice for you, others will sense a lack of commitment. The more you give, the more you will feel like getting out and asking others to join you in a sacrificial effort.

A board member from Ellis, Kansas said, "When I decided to give $1,000 to the library, I was committed! I became a tiger at asking people for money."

ASKING IS THE KEY

If you don't ask for the gift, people won't know what you want. Ken, my car salesman friend, could have sold the car the first hour, but he didn't ask the man to buy until 13 hours later. From Ken's actions the customer could have had the impression that all Ken wanted to do was to show him the car and drive around the countryside in it.

When you meet with a prospect, a normal opening might be to discuss the benefits of the library to the community. You might even discuss the merits of your new building or your automated circulation system. If you never ask for a contribution, your donor may think you are there for a friendly visit or to chat about the library.

How many times have you been in a situation where you had to communicate a difficult message? You thought you had stated what you wanted the other person to do, but a friend who was with you confirmed later that you didn't come right out and say what you wanted. Say, "We would like you to give $5,000 to the library building fund." It's helpful to take someone with you when contacting a major donor. Together you can be sure to ask for the gift.

GETTING TO YES

What do you say when asking for a gift? Ask for a specific amount. Be direct. Ask for the money with strong verbs such as: give, donate, or contribute. Don't ask, "Would you consider making a generous donation?" Your prospective donor can say "yes" to that question without giving a dime. He considered it and the answer is no!

Here are a few ways to ask for a gift.

- Please give. . .
- Won't you please help?
- The future of the library lies in your hands.
- You can make the difference.
- This is your chance to help. . .
- With your help, we can go on.
- Help us reach our goal.

THE POWER OF SILENCE

After you ask for the donation, be silent. This is one of the most critical pieces of advice in this book. After presenting your case—perhaps asking, "Will you help us reach our goal by giving $5,000?"—don't say another word until the donor has spoken. Researchers have learned that the average silence in any conversation is less than three seconds. Learn to be comfortable with the silence. Let your prospect speak next. If your donor says, "No," don't give up.

Listen!

She will probably tell you why she is turning you down. Try to find out why the answer is no. Agree with her, then point out another benefit of giving. She may feel that you are on her side. Sometimes you have to prove that you are seriously committed to your cause. Tell her you have already given $1,000. Now it is her turn.

Don't give up with the first "No." Keep listening and talking. She may change her mind. If you don't get the gift don't be disappointed. You have still learned something. You probably failed to predict the donor's capacity to give (how much discretionary cash she has) or her interest in the library.

Getting the donor to say yes may require several ploys, but it could be as simple as asking her, "What can I do to get you to say yes?" Maybe she will tell you about a benefit that you haven't thought of, or maybe the library is doing something that irritates her, such as having the book drop in an inconvenient place. If you can fix it, you may be in line for a nice gift.

What if she still says no?

Listen to her. Agree with her. Listen for clues that might give you a lead to a benefit that will make her want to give. Chances are good that she will give you several reasons for not giving. By listening carefully you will learn what is important to her. The connection between a benefit of your project and your prospect's needs is the key to getting the gift.

Don't give up with the first visit. If you fail at the first try, try again or send someone else in a few days. A fundraising rule of thumb is that it takes seven askings to get to yes. Your donor may change her mind after thinking about your request.

WHEN THE ECONOMY IS BAD

Sometimes we are afraid to ask for money because the economy is on a downswing. We are concerned that people don't feel they have money for necessities, much less luxuries—such as donations to our cause. Generally, the argument is not valid. The economy seems to have no bearing on what people give. Giving to charity has maintained an upward curve regardless of a bad economy or reduction in government support. Think of it this way: if you don't ask for a contribution for the library, someone else will ask for their organization.

They win! You lose! It's that simple.

People give small amounts (up to about $50) from regular discretionary income. Most people give large amounts from their assets. So it doesn't matter what the economy is like. If they have money in the bank and they want to give to your cause, they will give regardless of how many businesses are going broke on Main Street.

Some people don't have immediate access to their assets. When the donor says he can't give $1,000 right now, but he will give you $500. Say thank you and suggest that he might give another $500 later on. It is possible that his money is tied up in a certificate of deposit that will mature in the next few months. Go back and see him in three months.

ASKING FOR A PLEDGE

You ask for a pledge when it becomes obvious that the donors assets are tied up or he has no liquid assets to give at this time. About half of all fundraising comes in the form of pledges over a three- to five-year period. A pledge is usually based on anticipated discretionary income. Whatever the pledge is, accept it. A pledge of $1,000 over the next 12 months is better than a no gift at all.

DO YOUR HOMEWORK

In a small town, everyone knows everyone else. It won't take a 20-minute brainstorming session to learn the name of the richest person in town. But brainstorming is an effective technique for discovering the best people to ask in your community. You might also try:

Proxy statements for public held companies: These are avail-

"BE" ATTITUDES OF FUNDRAISING

Be committed. If you aren't going to give it your full commitment, don't do it. When you eat, drink, and sleep fundraising for your library, everyone who talks to you will know it.

Be friendly. Friends give to friends.

Be positive. Your attitude is infectious.

Be confident. When you ask for a gift, you can only win or break even. The only way you lose is by not asking.

Be bold and nice. Boldness without being nice is "pushy." Twisting someone's arm until they give may get the gift, but what about the next time? Goodwill is an intangible asset.

Be firm. Learn how to deal with objections. Most people have to get used to the idea of giving away money. It usually takes asking seven times to get the gift. Don't give up on the first "no."

Be knowledgeable. Know the benefits of your organization to the public in general and to the donor in particular. Point them out.

Be considerate of your donor. You donor has already given you a chunk of her time. Don't waste it. Make your pitch. Ask for the money. Get it. Say thank you and leave.

able from the Securities Exchange Commission. You may uncover people who have large amounts of stock they may be willing to donate to the library

Probate records: Ask for will inventory. The survivors may be interested in making a sizable memorial contribution.

Financial statements in divorces: Someone may have a chunk of money they would donate.

Country club list: Those who belong to country clubs often have more discretionary income to give away.

Retirement centers: People over 60 are some of the best givers—especially to libraries.

Trying one or more of these possibilities may uncover an untapped major source of benevolence.

SAY THANK YOU APPROPRIATELY

Saying thank you is the most obvious principle of all. The biggest question is: How do I match my thank you with the size of the gift? Your thank you could range from a simple note to someone who gave you a $100, to an elaborate reception honoring a gift large enough to build the entire new addition. The most important thing about saying thank you is to do it.

Saying thank you not only makes your donor feel good; it also makes you feel good. It may be the only "return on investment" your donor will receive. Sometimes fundraising groups have a big bash at the end of the campaign for all the workers and the donors who gave $1,000 or more. It is a good opportunity to give public recognition to workers and donors alike. But how can you recognize a large gift from a donor who wishes to remain anonymous? A quiet meal in a fancy restaurant might work fine. Anyone who gives anything to your campaign deserves a thank you.

THE RIGHT ATTITUDE

Soliciting funds is intimidating to almost everyone. The only reason we would even consider it is that we are firmly committed to the organization we support. A positive attitude is the key to overcoming our fears. I would rather look forward to being thin than to think of being on a diet. It's just less stressful. The list of "Be" Attitudes of Fundraising can help you feel positive about asking others for money.

Exercise

PRODDING THE BOARD

When board members balk at giving money, prepare to respond by using the following exercise:

List five reasons why board members should contribute to the library.

Give five responses the board could have to these reasons.

Tell five ways you could respond to their rebuttal.

Who should ask? "Volunteers," is generally the right answer. They are the heart of any fundraising effort. But there are times when the chief executive (the librarian) can have a pivotal role in soliciting a large gift. He or she could accompany the chair of the fundraising committee to answer questions and provide moral support. Volunteers who have made a donation are the most effective fundraisers in your community.

Whether you use a professional fundraiser or not, you need committed, well-trained volunteers with connections at all levels of the community—especially the levels with most of the money.

First of all, you may not want everyone who says "I'll do it!" to be on your fundraising team. Some people will do the right thing for the wrong reason. It is better to work with a few highly committed people than to work with an army of workers for whom other things have a higher priority. So it is wise to look at why people want to join your fundraising campaign. Be cautious if they are doing it simply to foster a better image for themselves or their business, or as a company requirement. Did a friend twist their arm? If your volunteers are motivated by reasons like these, their commitment will be less the 100 percent. Rather, look for those who have a sense of community service, who have proven skills and knowledge to offer, and who feel the importance of your cause. These reasons are conducive to commitment.

What greater measurement of commitment can you find for a fundraising committee than a willingness to give money to the cause? Beware of people who will give their time but not their money. They will lack the commitment to produce the results you need.

TRANSFORMING VOLUNTEERS INTO FUNDRAISERS.

If you already have a group of hardworking volunteers, you may be tempted to convert them into fundraisers.

Be careful!

It may not work!

Some people would rather wash windows or clean bathrooms than go out and ask for money. A trustee on one of the boards I work with is a medical doctor. He would rather mow the library's lawn himself than raise the money to pay someone else to do it. Almost all library trustees felt that fundraising was *not* one of their major responsibilities, according to my survey of library boards in the Central Kansas Library System.

We can make effective use of regular library trustees if we understand their needs. Trustees in small public libraries worry about:

- their own commitment to fundraising
- community support
- selecting the right project
- finding the right leadership
- planning and organizing the effort
- recruiting and training volunteers to solicit and
- securing support of city officials.

If you are going to secure the help of your board, you will have to address these concerns.

CONVINCING THE BOARD

Library trustees are usually volunteers. Even though they tend to discount their fundraising role, they can be good at asking others for money if they understand the library's need. You might try a survey to get them moving. Ask board members a variety of questions regarding what they would like the library to be. Then ask, "Can the library be all of these things to our patrons the way it is now?" This may help them see the light, but if they aren't committed, there is very little a librarian or a lone board member can do.

Once the library board commits itself to a fundraising project, everyone should be asked to give. A trustee might say, "I give my time and effort to this cause. Isn't that enough? Why should I have to give money too?" The answer is simple. Time and money are not the same thing. If board members are committed enough to your library to give their time, they should be committed enough to give their money, too.

SUMMARY

Once we understand the nature of our task it is easier accomplish it. People can raise money for their library by doing just about anything they can imagine and implement. They will make more money with less effort if they apply the principles of fundraising and sound selling. Asking for the gift—"making the close"—is the key to the success of every fundraising activity.

3 SELECTING THE ACTIVITY

Our job as fundraisers is to "create the desire to give; then to give generously; then to give recurringly; then to give ultimately by bequest."

Arthur Frantzreb,
author and professional fundraising consultant

Keep this quote in mind as you consider every fundraising activity. It will focus your mind on the goal of raising money for your library. Anything that does not move your prospective donors to the desire to give, to give generously, recurringly, and, ultimately, by bequest, should be discarded.

I remember as a child, selling dance tickets for the PTA. We lived in a rural area, so I rode my bicycle all over the school district asking people if they wanted to buy a PTA dance ticket. That was the only fundraising activity they had ever had. The year my mother was PTA president, we had a carnival. Wow! It was great fun for families.

Today there is a plethora of ideas for raising money. In this chapter we will examine a variety of techniques and discuss how to select the right activity for a given project.

Fundraising as the catalyst

The number-one goal of the library leaders I work with is to get more people to use the library. Librarians and trustees feel trapped because they don't know what to do to make their services more attractive. Fundraising can be the catalyst. Sometimes a little shot in the arm can result in big changes.

Why do you become involved in fundraising in the first place? Because normal channels of revenue are not adequate to meet the library needs of the community. You probably need more money for one of six basic reasons:

1. You want money for a new library. The amount you need may be as much as ten times your annual budget.
2. You need almost as much money to remodel your present facility.
3. You need more money than you can get from your normal operating budget for an important piece of equipment, such as a computer.

4. You need extra money to support special programs, such as family film night or a special guest storyteller.
5. You need more money for normal operations. You aren't receiving enough from your municipality to fund everyday programs.
6. You need more money for books. Doesn't every library?

You may be able to think of a financial need I haven't mentioned, but it will probably fit it into one of the categories.

How do you fund these needs? You probably wouldn't mount a major campaign to buy a typewriter. Neither would you try to raise $1,000,000 for a new building with bake sales. Everything you do will help, but for big-dollar projects you need big-dollar techniques, some of which are mentioned on the charts beginning on page 48.

Major sources of library funding.

Funding for libraries usually comes from two sources—taxes and fundraising. In fact, the best way to increase the revenue for a library is to raise taxes. However, it may not be the first. M. P. Marchant, Professor of Library Science at Brigham Young University, says, "Fundraising efforts are important because of their emotional impact in support of tax initiatives." Library fundraising projects, by their nature, create a higher level of visibility for the library. People who will give even $5 to a fundraising effort are more likely to vote in favor of a library bond issue or a mill levy increase. Fundraising itself is a public relations activity. So, try a few fundraising activities before you go for a tax referendum.

Before we go too far, we need to distinguish fundraising from money-making projects. Fundraising is asking people for a gift. There may be a few tangible benefits involved such as lunch with the board or an invitation to auction, but basically you are asking for a gift. With money-making projects, you are selling something for its approximate value. Some people would rather sell candy or chances on a quilt than ask for money. Others prefer to simply ask for a gift. You have to be in tune with your volunteers and your community to make the right decision on this issue. But as you will see from the charts, making things and selling them will never produce the large amounts of money you need to build a new library. These activities will supplement the big dollars that have to come from solicitation of gifts.

Matching ideas to community needs

Your job as a fundraiser is to bring together the needs of the library and needs or values of individuals in your community. It may be as simple as sitting down with a committee and making two lists. Head one list: "What does the library need?" At the top of the other list, write: "What does the community need?" Where answers converge you have a common point of concern and the basis for helping each other.

Economic development was the hot topic in Kansas in the late 1980s. Many libraries positioned themselves to provide information to the community and business leaders on the topic. Libraries became the allies of business.

Matching needs may be as simple as publishing a telephone directory. In Prairie View, Kansas (population 123), library fundraisers discovered that although the residents in three nearby towns could call each other toll-free, they had no unified telephone directory. With a little help from others, they published a directory and sold copies to the local residents in each of the towns. When a fundraising group is able to focus on a community need and make money by filling it, they are well on their way to success.

STRUCTURE FOR MATCHING NEEDS

As you consider what to do to raise the money, start by looking at your needs and matching them to the most appropriate fundraising activity. Fundraising possibilities generally fall into one of the following:

A major campaign. This is a one-shot effort over a short period of time to bring in a lot of cash and pledges for a new library—sometimes to fund an endowment, the interest from which will be used to subsidize ongoing services.

Long-term or planned giving. These are gifts from people who want to provide for the library after they no longer need their money.

General solicitation. Asking individuals for money is the mainstay of fundraising.

Special-event solicitation. Public television's annual fund drive leads the list in this category.

Grants. Project grants from foundations and the federal government are potential sources if you know how to write grant proposals.

Local governments. Taxes are the best way, over time, to get more money for your library.

Collecting coupons. Some people will save labels from soup or canned goods for cash rather than go out and knock on doors asking for money.

In-kind gifts. An office products store might give a typewriter to the library in lieu of a cash contribution.

Sell something. To some people, fundraising is more palatable if the contributor is asked to buy a product. Selling something is also a good way get money from non-constituents.

Contract for service. Labor is exchanged for money which goes to the organization. It can be anything from washing windows or cars to performing as a clown at a birthday party,

Sell something you buy. In essence you become a retail agent for a producer.

Sell something you make with materials you buy. With your labor, you convert raw materials into a saleable product.

Sell something made with donated materials. The ubiquitous bake sale leads this list.

Sell donated items. Donors give you items to sell rather than giving cash. Benefit auctions and rummage sales are in this group.

Sell something on commission. Your fundraising group becomes a retail agent earning a percentage of the cost of each unit sold.

Sell the opportunity to sell. Others have products they want to sell. You create the forum and attract buyers.

Special events. People enjoy them, but they are a lot of work. They usually generate more goodwill than money for your project.

Special guests. An author or other dignitary can give your project great visibility.

Performances. Benefit concerts by name performers will draw a large crowd, but unless they donate their services it may not be worth it.

Contests. Your donors pay a fee to compete in a sporting event. The winners get a trophy and a small cash prize, and you get the rest.

Community fun. People enjoy getting together to have fun. You can please them and make money at the same time.

Gambling. Bingo and card parties can be fun. Make sure they are legal in your state before trying it.

You have probably tried several activities that are not on the list, but they would probably fit into one of the general categories I have listed.

The next step is to match a need with an activity. The matrix of recommended activities to meet various library needs will help you match your need to the type fundraising activity best suited for your community.

You will notice on the following charts that I don't recommend very many selling activities for a building fund or remodeling project. While every dollar counts, these projects do not raise enough money to complete such a major undertaking. However, I know of a newspaper drive that has gone on for more than 14 years. The money has built several fine buildings for the 4-H fairgrounds in Barton County, Kansas. No other agency in the area even tries to have a paper drive. The 4-H people have it well in hand—earning over $5,000 a year. The recycling people who bought the paper said that they were the most well-organized group they had ever worked with. It all depends on the community.

You will also notice that I don't recommend very many activities to supplement operations. I believe that library operations should be funded from tax dollars. If a library has trouble meeting its operational budget, it should seek additional funds from tax sources—through either legislation or a referendum.

Check with local and state laws regarding fundraising activities involving gambling. Be sure the community will accept gambling before you use it. Never spend more in prizes than you expect to take in.

Potential and Needs of Fundraising Activities

Fundraising Activities	Return on investment of time and effort	Potential for more than $10 per capita	Need for many volunteers	Need for special training for volunteers	Need for up-front cash compared to possible income	Need for specialized outside help
Money Gifts						
Major Campaign						
Endowment fund drive	High	High	Medium	High	Medium	High
Building fund drive	High	High	High	High	High	High
Annual fund drive	High	High	High	Medium	Medium	Initially yes
Unsolicited gifts	Uncertain	High	None	None	None	None
Long Term, Planned Giving						
Bequests	Long wait?	Medium	Low	High	Low	High
Insurance policies	Long wait?	Sometimes	Low	High	Low	High
Charitable trusts	High	Medium	Low	High	Low	High
Memorial gifts (books)	High	Low	Low	Low	Low	Low
Memorial gifts (equipment)	High	Medium	Low	Low	Low	Low
General Solicitation						
Direct mail	Very Low	Low	Low	Low	High	It depends
Telephone	Medium	Medium	High	Medium	High	Low
Sell memberships	High	Low	High	Medium	Low	Low
Door-to-door	High	Medium	Very High	Medium	Low	Low
Business and industry	High	It depends	Low	Medium	Low	Medium
Civic groups	High	Low	None	None	None	None
Service clubs	Medium	Low	None	None	None	None
Special Event Solicitation						
Telethon (TV)	Low	Low	High	High	High	Very High
Radiothon	Medium	Low	High	Medium	Medium	High
Walkathon	High	Low	Very High	Low	Low	Medium
Readathon	Medium	Low	Very High	Low	Low	Low
Grants						
Private foundations	High	It depends	Low	Low	None	Good idea
Civic club foundations	High	Medium	Low	Low	Varies	Good idea
Corporate foundations	High	High	Low	Low	Medium	Good idea
Matching grants	High	HIgh	Low	Low	High	Good idea
Federal grants	High	Medium	None	None	None	Good idea

Recommended Fundraising Activities to Meet Library Project Needs

Fundraising Activities	Funding for new building program	Funding for remodeling project	Funding for major equipment purchase	Funding to enhance programs	Funding to supplement operations	Funding to supplement book budget
Money Gifts						
Major Campaign						
Endowment fund drive	No	No	No	No	Use interest	Use interest
Building fund drive	Yes	Yes	Yes	No	No	No
Annual fund drive	No	Yes	Yes	No	Yes	Yes
Unsolicited gifts	Yes	Yes	Yes	Yes	Yes	Yes
Long Term, Planned Giving						
Bequests	Yes	Yes	Yes	No	No	Yes
Insurance policies	Yes	Yes	No	Yes	Yes	Yes
Charitable trusts	No	Yes	Yes	Yes	Yes	Yes
Memorial gifts (books)	No	No	No	No	No	Yes
Memorial gifts (equipment)	No	Yes	Yes	No	No	No
General solicitation						
Direct mail	Yes	Yes	Yes	Yes	No	Yes
Telephone	Yes	Yes	Yes	No	No	No
Sell Memberships	No	No	No	Yes	No	Yes
Door-to-door	Yes	Yes	Yes	Yes	No	Yes
Business and industry	Yes	Yes	Yes	Yes	No	Yes
Civic groups	Yes	Yes	Yes	Yes	No	Yes
Service clubs	Yes	Yes	Yes	Yes	No	Yes
Special Event solicitation						
Telethon (TV)	No	No	No	No	No	No
Radiothon	Yes	Yes	Yes	No	No	Yes
Walkathon	Yes	Yes	Yes	Yes	No	Yes
Readathon	No	No	Yes	Yes	No	Yes
Grants						
Private foundations	Yes	Yes	Yes	No	No	No
Civic foundations	Yes	Yes	Yes	No	No	No
Corporate foundations	Yes	Yes	Yes	No	No	No
Matching grants	Yes	Yes	Yes	Yes	No	No
Federal grants	Yes	Yes	Yes	Yes	No	No

Potential and Needs of Fundraising Activities

Fundraising Activities	Return on investment of time and effort	Potential for more than $10 per capita	Need for many volunteers	Need for special training for volunteers	Need for up-front cash compared to possible income	Need for specialized outside help
Local governments						
Bond elections	High	Very High	High	Medium	Medium	Medium
Referendums	High	Very High	High	Medium	Medium	Medium
Tax increases (legislatied)	High	Very High	Low	Low	Medium	Low
Grants	High	Medium	Low	Low	Low	High
Collecting/Coupons						
Promotional coupons	Medium	Very Low	Very High	None	Low	None
Percentage of receipts in stores	Medium	Low	Very High	None	Low	None
Saving labels	Medium	Low	Very High	None	Low	None
Recycling cans and bottles	Low	Very Low	Very High	None	Medium	None
Newspaper drive	Medium	Medium	Very High	None	Medium	Medium
In-Kind gifts.						
Open letter to Santa	High	Low	Low	None	Low	Medium
Refreshments for special events	High	Low	Low	Low	Low	Low
Rewards for children's prog.	High	None	Low	Low	Low	Low
Business--goods and services	High	Medium	Low	Low	Low	Low
Sell Something						
Contracts for services						
Washing windows	Medium	Low	Medium	Meduim	Medium	Low
Parking cars	High	Low	Low	Meduim	Low	Low
Inventory work	HIgh	Low	Medium	Meduim	Low	Low
Cleaning new homes	Medium	Low	Medium	Low	Medium	Low
Mow lawns	Medium	Low	Low	Low	Medium	Low
Baby sit	Low	None	Medium	Meduim	Low	Low
Car washes	Medium	Low	Low	Low	Medium	Low
Speakers bureau	HIgh	Low	Medium	High	Medium	Goodidea
Rent-a-grandparent	High	Low	Medium	Low	Low	Low
Answer telephone	Medium	Low	Medium	High	High	Low
House sitting	Medium	Low	Low	Low	Low	Low
Special programs	Medium	Low	Medium	Meduim	Medium	Low
Handyman	Medium	Low	Medium	High	High	Low
Play Santa	Low	Low	Low	Medium	High	Low

Recommended Fundraising Activities to Meet Library Project Needs

Fundraising Activities	Funding for new building program	Funding for remodeling project	Funding for major equipment purchase	Funding to enhance programs	Funding to supplement operations	Funding to supplement book budget
Local governments						
Bond elections	Yes	Yes	Yes	No	No	No
Referendums	Yes	Yes	Yes	Yes	Yes	Yes
Tax increases (Legislated)	Yes	Yes	Yes	Yes	Yes	Yes
Grants	Yes	Yes	Yes	Yes	Yes	Yes
Collecting/Coupons						
Promotional coupons	No	No	Yes	Yes	No	Yes
Percentage of receipts in stores	Yes	Yes	Yes	Yes	No	Yes
Saving labels	Yes	Yes	Yes	Yes	No	Yes
Recycling cans and bottles	No	No	No	No	No	No
Newspaper drive	No	No	Yes	Yes	Yes	Yes
In-Kind gifts.						
Open letter to Santa	No	No	Yes	No	No	Yes
Refreshments for special events	No	No	Yes	No	No	Yes
Rewards for children's prog.	No	No	No	Yes	No	No
Business--goods and services	No	No	Yes	Yes	No	No
Sell Something						
Contracts for services						
Washing windows	No	No	Yes	No	No	Yes
Parking cars	No	No	Yes	No	No	Yes
Inventory work	No	No	Yes	Yes	No	Yes
Cleaning new homes	No	Yes	Yes	No	No	Yes
Mow lawns	No	No	Yes	No	No	Yes
Baby sit	No	No	Yes	No	No	Yes
Car washes	No	Yes	Yes	No	No	Yes
Speakers bureau	Yes	Yes	Yes	Yes	No	Yes
Rent-a-grandparent	No	Yes	Yes	No	No	Yes
Answer telephone	No	Yes	Yes	No	No	Yes
House sitting	No	Yes	Yes	No	No	Yes
Special programs	No	Yes	Yes	Yes	No	Yes
Handyman	No	Yes	Yes	Yes	No	Yes
Play Santa	No	No	Yes	Yes	No	Yes

Potential and Needs of Fundraising Activities

Fundraising Activities	Return on investment of time and effort	Potential for more than $10 per capita	Need for many volunteers	Need for special training for volunteers	Need for up-front cash compared to possible income	Need for specialized outside help
Clown service	Medium	Low	Low	High	Medium	Medium
Birthday grams	Medium	Low	Medium	Meduim	Medium	Low
Junior Friends workdays	Medium	Low	High	Meduim	Medium	Low
Sell something you buy to sell						
Candy	Low	Low	High	Medium	Sometimes	Medium
Light bulbs	Low	Low	High	Medium	Sometimes	Medium
Fruit cakes	Low	Low	High	Medium	Sometimes	Medium
Christmas cards	Low	Low	High	Medium	Sometimes	Medium
Friends logo item sale	Low	Low	Medium	Medium	Sometimes	Medium
Christmas tree sales	Low	Low	Medium	Medium	Sometimes	Medium
Made with purchased materials						
Soup supper	Medium	Low	Low	Medium	Sometimes	Medium
Cook book	Low	Low	High	Medium	Low	Publisher
Pizza party	Low	Low	High	Medium	Low	Medium
"Artistic" hot dog sale	Medium	Low	High	Medium	Medium	Medium
Food fair	Medium	Low	High	Medium	Sometimes	Medium
Made with donated materials						
Bake /Candy sales	High	Very Low	High	Low	Low	Low
Homemade bread	High	Very Low	Low	Low	Low	Low
Quilts	High	Very Low	High	Low	Low	Low
Bazaar items	High	Very Low	High	Low	Low	Low
Donation to sell						
Auctions (new goods)	High	Medium	Medium	Low	Low	Auctioneer
Attic auctions (used goods)	High	Medium	Medium	Low	Low	Auctioneer
Antique bazaar	High	Medium	Medium	Low	Medium	Low
Dutch auctions	High	Medium	Medium	Low	Medium	Low
Silent auction	High	Medium	Medium	Low	Low	Low
Garage sales	High	Medium	Medium	Low	Low	Low
Plant boutique	High	Medium	Medium	Low	Low	Low
Rummage sales	High	Medium	High	Low	Low	Low
Flower sales	High	Medium	Medium	Low	Low	Low
Thrift and gift shops	High	Medium	Medium	Low	High	Low

Recommended Fundraising Activities to Meet Library Project Needs

Fundraising Activities	Funding for new building program	Funding for remodeling project	Funding for major equipment purchase	Funding to enhance programs	Funding to supplement operations	Funding to supplement book budget
Clown service	No	No	Yes	Yes	No	Yes
Birthday grams	No	No	Yes	Yes	No	Yes
Junior Friends workdays	No	No	Yes	Yes	No	Yes
Sell something you buy						
Candy	No	No	No	Yes	No	Yes
Light bulbs	No	No	No	Yes	No	Yes
Fruit cakes	No	No	No	Yes	No	Yes
Christmas cards	No	No	Yes	Yes	No	Yes
Friends logo item sale	No	No	Yes	Yes	No	Yes
Christmas tree sales	No	No	Yes	Yes	No	Yes
Made with purchased materials						
Soup suppers	No	Yes	Yes	Yes	No	Yes
Cook book	Yes	Yes	Yes	Yes	No	Yes
Pizza party	No	No	Yes	Yes	No	Yes
"Artistic" hot dog sale	No	No	Yes	Yes	No	Yes
Food fair	No	Yes	Yes	Yes	No	Yes
Made with donated materials						
Bake /Candy sales	No	No	Yes	Yes	No	Yes
Homemade bread	No	No	Yes	Yes	No	Yes
Quilts	No	No	No	Yes	No	Yes
Bazaar items	No	No	No	Yes	No	Yes
Donations to sell						
Auctions (new goods)	Yes	Yes	Yes	Yes	Yes	Yes
Attic auctions (used goods)	No	Yes	Yes	Yes	No	Yes
Antique bazaar	No	No	Yes	Yes	No	Yes
Dutch auction	No	No	Yes	Yes	No	Yes
Silent auction	No	No	Yes	Yes	No	Yes
Garage sales	No	No	Yes	Yes	No	Yes
Plant boutique	No	No	No	Yes	No	Yes
Rummage sales	No	No	Yes	Yes	No	Yes
Flower sales	No	No	No	Yes	No	Yes
Thrift and gift shops	No	No	Yes	Yes	No	Yes

Potential and Needs of Fundraising Activities

Fundraising Activities	Return on investment of time and effort	Potential for more than $10 per capita	Need for many volunteers	Need for special training for volunteers	Need for up-front cash compared to possible income	Need for specialized outside help
Rent videos	Low	Low	Medium	Medium	High	Medium
Used book sale	Low	Medium	High	Low	Low	Low
Sell something on Commission						
Pizza	High	Low	High	Medium	Low	Low
Photography deals	High	Low	High	Medium	Low	Low
Tickets to local events	High	Low	High	Medium	Low	Low
Sell the opportunity to sell						
Craft classes-craft items	Medium	Low	Low	Low	High	Low
Crafts boutique	Medium	Low	Low	Low	High	Low
Children's book fair	Medium	Low	Medium	Low	Low	Low
Dollhouse show	Medium	Low	Low	Low	Low	Low
Farmers market	Medium	Low	Low	Low	Medium	Low
Flea market	Medium	Low	Low	Low	Low	Low
Swap meets	Medium	Low	Low	Low	Low	Low
Special Events						
Special Guests						
Author functions	Low	Low	Low	Low	Low	High
Dinners with guest speakers	Can vary	Medium	Low	Low	High	High
Benefit dinner/dance	Can vary	Medium	Low	Low	Low	High
Performances						
Concerts	Varies	Low	High	Medium	Sometimes	High
Fashion show	Medium	Low	High	Medium	High	High
Film festivals	Low	Low	Low	Low	High	High
Rodeos	Low	Low	High	Low	High	High
Talent show	Low	Low	High	High	Medium	High
Theatre Parties	Low	Low	High	Low	Low	High
Bus trips	Low	Low	Low	Low	High	High

Recommended Fundraising Activities to Meet Library Project Needs

Fundraising Activities	Funding for new building program	Funding for remodeling project	Funding for major equipment purchase	Funding to enhance programs	Funding to supplement operations	Funding to supplement book budget
Rent videos	No	No	Yes	Yes	No	Yes
Used book sale	No	No	Yes	Yes	No	Yes
Sell something on Commission						
Pizza	No	No	No	No	No	No
Photography deals	No	No	No	No	No	No
Tickets to local events	No	No	No	No	No	No
Sell the opportunity to sell						
Craft classes	No	No	No	Yes	No	Yes
Crafts boutique	No	No	Yes	Yes	No	Yes
Children's book fair	No	No	Yes	Yes	No	Yes
Dollhouse show	No	No	Yes	Yes	No	Yes
Farmers market	No	No	No	Yes	No	Yes
Flea market	No	No	Yes	Yes	No	Yes
Swap meets	No	No	Yes	Yes	No	Yes
Special Events						
Special Guests						
Author functions	No	No	No	Yes	No	Yes
Dinners with guest speakers	Yes	Yes	Yes	Yes	No	Yes
Benefit dinner/dance	No	Yes	Yes	Yes	No	Yes
Performances						
Concerts	No	No	No	Yes	No	No
Fashion show	No	Yes	Yes	Yes	No	Yes
Film festivals	No	No	No	Yes	No	No
Rodeos	Yes	Yes	Yes	Yes	No	Yes
Talent show	Yes	Yes	Yes	Yes	No	Yes
Theatre Parties	No	Yes	Yes	Yes	No	Yes
Bus trips	No	Yes	Yes	Yes	No	Yes

Potential and Needs of Fundraising Activities

Fundraising Activities	Return on investment of time and effort	Potential for more than $10 per capita	Need for many volunteers	Need for special training for volunteers	Need for up-front cash compared to possible income	Need for specialized outside help
Contests						
Fishing tournaments	High	Low	Medium	Medium	Medium	High
Golf tournaments	High	Low	Medium	High	Medium	High
Kiss-the-pig contest	High	Low	High	Medium	Low	Low
Tractor pulls	High	Low	Low	High	High	High
Community fun						
Luau	Medium	Low	Medium	Low	High	Medium
Block party	High	Low	High	Low	Medium	Low
Carnival	Medium	Low	High	Low	Medium	Medium
Street dances	Medium	Low	Medium	Low	Medium	High
Home tours	High	Low	Low	Low	Low	Low
Garden tours	High	Low	Low	Low	Low	Medium
Pancake feed	High	Low	High	Low	High	Medium
Gambling						
Card parties	High	Low	Medium	Low	Low	Low
Bingo	High	Medium	High	Low	High	High
Casino night	High	Low	High	Low	High	High
Casino trips	High	Low	Medium	Low	High	High
Raffles	High	Low	High	Low	Medium	High

Recommended Fund-raising activities to meet library project needs

Fundraising Activities	Funding for new building program	Funding for remodeling project	Funding for major equipment purchase	Funding to enhance programs	Funding to supplement operations	Funding to supplement book budget
Contests						
Fishing tournaments	No	No	Yes	Yes	No	Yes
Golf tournaments	Yes	Yes	Yes	Yes	No	Yes
Kiss-the-pig contest	No	No	Yes	Yes	No	Yes
Tractor pulls	Yes	Yes	Yes	Yes	No	Yes
Community fun						
Luau	Yes	Yes	Yes	Yes	No	Yes
Block party	No	No	Yes	Yes	No	Yes
Carnival	No	No	Yes	Yes	No	Yes
Street dances	No	No	Yes	Yes	No	Yes
Home tours	Yes	Yes	Yes	Yes	No	Yes
Garden tours	Yes	Yes	Yes	Yes	No	Yes
Pancake feed	No	Yes	Yes	Yes	No	Yes
Gambling						
Card parties	Yes	Yes	Yes	Yes	No	Yes
Bingo	Yes	Yes	Yes	Yes	Yes	Yes
Casino night	Yes	Yes	Yes	Yes	Yes	Yes
Casino trips	Yes	Yes	Yes	Yes	Yes	Yes
Raffles	No	Yes	Yes	Yes	No	Yes

SIX POINTS

Before you launch a fundraising project, you may want to review the potential and needs of various fundraising activities. I have taken the same list of fundraising activities and made comments on the appropriateness of each on six points:

Return on investment of time and effort: One of the librarians I interviewed said, "I read lots of articles on how to raise money, but they all seem to be too much work for the small amount of money you make. What I need is an idea that will make a lot of money." Everyone's time is limited. You don't want to waste it on activities that won't get you the money you need to do the job.

Potential for more than $10 per capita: If you are going to build a new library, you will need about $10 per person living in your service area. Don't waste your time on bake sales and collecting aluminum cans.

Need for many volunteers: Some fundraising projects require more people than others. Sometimes a few well connected solicitors are more effective than an army of volunteers knocking on every door in town. Recruiting many volunteers is also good public relations for your campaign. Balance the two.

Need for special training for volunteers: It doesn't take much training for volunteers to go out and collect aluminum cans, but if you want them to telephone people to solicit for the library's building fund you will need a high level of training. Your ability to train your volunteers may affect the fundraising activity you select.

Need for up front cash: This category asks the question, "Can we afford to do this?" Or, "Can we afford to risk the money we already have?" If a project takes a lot of "seed money" and you are already operating on a shoestring, maybe you should try another activity first.

Need for specialized outside help: Professional fundraising consultants can help you get started and organize your volunteers in a way that will produce better results than if you tried to do it on your own. (For more detailed information on consultants see Chapter 15.) A professional auctioneer is a must for an auction. It is a good idea to have the services of an experienced grant writer if you want your grant to be funded.

The preceding charts are designed to help you evaluate the potential of each fundraising activity based on these criteria. They can help you match your project need with a fundraising activity, and match your resources with an activity. Together they give you an objective way to look at fundraising for a small public library. The real test comes when you sit down with your fundraising group and brainstorm. Your job is to figure out what will work best in your community.

If I were invited to consult with someone in a small public library on raising money for their town, I would suggest they consider several of the following fundraising techniques.

FAVORITE FUNDRAISING TECHNIQUES

Direct mail campaigns: This is a good way to build a solid donor base. The first year you might break even, but after that it gets more profitable.

Used book sale: Libraries are a natural for this one. I wouldn't recommend this for any organization, except a library. Make it big!

An auction: One big push, then it is over. It nets a lot of money in a short period and everyone has a good time.

Capital fund drives: Conduct a feasibility study first to make sure you have the goodwill of the community. If you don't have it, get it before you try. People will give more to a one-time request than a regular solicitation.

Door-to-door solicitation: In a small town asking people for money face-to-face doesn't take too many workers, and it works well.

Memorial and deferred giving: People are looking for an appropriate way to preserve the memory of a loved one and invest in the future of the community.

Tax referenda: This is the most effective way, over time, to increase your library's budget. If this is not an option in your state, lobby until you get it.

Annual events: People get used to the library having its annual book fair and craft show on the last Saturday in July.

Special events: While they are a lot of work and may not generate much money, they bring goodwill and visibility to the library.

SUMMARY

Small libraries seem to have the backing of everyone in the community. You can do anything you want when you have the support of the whole town. You just have to work with the community and library leaders to figure out what will work best where you live and give it a try.

4 PLANNING

"Strategic planning is worthless—unless there is first a strategic vision. A strategic vision is a clear image of what you want to achieve, which then organizes and instructs every step toward that goal. The extraordinarily successful strategic vision for NASA was 'Put a man on the moon by the end of the decade.' That strategic vision gave magnetic direction to the entire organization. Nobody had to be told or reminded of where the organization was going."

John Naisbitt, *Megatrends*

Vision is the heart and soul of every fundraising plan. What is the vision for your library? More specifically, what is your vision for your library. If every member of your team has the same vision for your library and you are willing to work, there is every reason that your plan will succeed.

You want your library to have more money than it has right now. You want people to get what they want when they come to your library. Perhaps they can't do it in your library with things they way they are now. You may be stuck in a library that was built in 1912. Some people in the community are as old as your library and can't climb the 11 steps to the front door. If they could get inside, they would find it so crowded they could barely turn around. If that is the way it is, you want a new building.

Go for it!

You want more for your library than a roof that doesn't leak and a warm place for people to come in winter. You want to expand the vision of your community through high-tech equipment and up-to-date materials. Children are using computers every day—not as toys, but as tools for speedier access to information. You want more for your library just so it can reach more people in the community. Are you the one who sets the vision for your library?

Why not shoot for the moon?

President John Kennedy set the vision for NASA in a speech given on May 25, 1961 when he said, "This nation should commit itself to achieving the goal, before this decade is out, of landing a man on the moon and returning him safely to earth." While you are not going to the moon, the task before you may seem just as awesome. You can accomplish it, just as NASA did. If you can write it down, you can do it.

Let's take a look at NASA's vision. *Put a man on the moon and return him safely to earth in this decade.* It contains three elements that are crucial to attaining all goals:

1. It states what was to be done.

2. It was measurable.

3. It had a date for accomplishment.

This goal uses 15 words. Let's see if we can write a goal (create a vision) for your library that meets the same requirements—state what is to be done, make it measurable, and set a completion date. How does this sound? *Raise $400,000 through public contributions for a new library by 18 months from today.* In fourteen words we have created a vision that is specific, measurable within a fixed time frame.

What happens when we write down a goal like raising $400,000? The problem is turned over to the subconscious mind. Things begin to fall into place. We meet people. We read something or write it. Thoughts come to our mind. All these processes move us steadily toward our goal.

Your goal may not be as lofty as putting a man on the moon, raising $400,000, or writing a book. It may be as simple as carpeting the children's room of the library. Can you see the carpet? What color is it? Can you feel the texture? Can you touch its softness under your feet? Can you see children lying on it, reading? If you can, you can have it. If you can get others to catch the same vision, you can have it sooner. The key to fundraising is creating a vision and having other people share it.

Once, while conducting a workshop for library trustees, I asked one of them what her vision for her library was. She said, "I see a brand-new library."

I said, "What does it look like? What does it have in it.?"

She responded, "I see two rest rooms. One for women and one for men—both accessible to the handicapped."

I asked what else she saw.

She said, "I see a comfortable, quiet place to sit and read magazines."

As I pursued her vision for the library with her, she told me more of what she saw. Then I said, "If you can write it down, you can have it." Somehow putting it down on paper changes the level of commitment. The difference between a wish and a goal is a number and a date—written down on paper.

NEED FOR PLANNING

We have looked at brainstorming and creating a vision as precursors to planning. Now it's time to look at planning as a process. There are many good books on planning. One of the best I have seen is *Managing Change: A How-To-Do-It Manual for Planning, Implementing and Evaluating Change in Libraries,* by Susan C. Curzon (Neal-Schuman Publishers, 1989). If you will plug your fundraising project into the model she uses, you will have a successful project.

The purpose of planning is to organize, manage, and control change in a way that meets the needs of the organization. Fundraising is creating change. You are changing the location or purpose of other people's money in a way that will benefit your library.

The first job of any planning group is to assess the current need. You do this by asking: Where are we now? What are our concerns? What is occurring? To whom? How often? So what? Does it really matter?

If the roof leaks and some people can't climb the 11 steps of your old library building, it makes a difference. If there is no room on the shelves for even one more book, it really matters. Your job is to figure out what matters most in your library and do something about it.

The need for a new, updated, or remodeled building seems to be the target of most library fundraising. Most libraries "get by" or "make do" with the revenue they receive from taxes and the few unsolicited gifts that come in. Even though these funds may be inadequate, general operation and maintenance of the library is handled with the money available. The big-ticket items, such as a building project (new, remodeled, expanded, or a major repair) often set a fundraising effort in motion. A library board can muddle through for years wishing they had a new library, and one day a new board member will open the eyes of the others by saying, "We need a new library." Wheels start to turn, things start to happen.

It is one thing to say, "We need a new library," and another to realize exactly what it entails. Following is a worksheet that will help you assess your building needs.

Completing this worksheet will help you pinpoint your needs. You might even ask a few patrons to fill out the worksheet. They will help you see your library from a different perspective.

Let's say your library is new enough and it doesn't need repairs.

BUILDING NEEDS ANALYSIS WORKSHEET

		Yes	No	Comments
PLANT EXTERIOR				
	Inviting/appealing	___	___	_____
	Meets fire codes	___	___	_____
	Roof in good condition	___	___	_____
	Energy Efficiency			
	Ceiling insulated	___	___	_____
	Walls insulated	___	___	_____
	Windows efficient	___	___	_____
	Doors efficient	___	___	_____
	Foundation			
	Structurally sound	___	___	_____
	Moisture proof	___	___	_____
	Proper drainage	___	___	_____
	Entrances/Exits			
	Easy to open/close	___	___	_____
	All weather (covered)	___	___	_____
	Easily accessed (stairs)	___	___	_____
	Location			
	High traffic area	___	___	_____
	Available to mass transit	___	___	_____
	Adequate parking	___	___	_____
	Handicapped Parking	___	___	_____
	Well lit at night	___	___	_____
	Visibility			
	Effective signing	___	___	_____
	Hours visible from street	___	___	_____
	"Library" in 4+ inch letters	___	___	_____
PLANT INTERIOR	Heating and cooling			
	Good condition	___	___	_____
	Energy efficient	___	___	_____
	Humidity control	___	___	_____
	Flooring, Walls and Ceiling			
	Good condition	___	___	_____
	Acoustical	___	___	_____
	Exude pleasantness	___	___	_____
	Basic Layout			
	Aids traffic flow	___	___	_____
	Handicapped access	___	___	_____

		Yes	No	Comments

PLANT INTERIOR

All areas controllable
Elevator for multi-levels
Rest Rooms
Handicapped access
Child access
Controllable
Electrical and Lighting
   Under 10 years
   AV and cable support
   Computer support
   Phone and modem support
   Adequate outlets
   Suitable lighting all areas
   100 ft. candle in study areas

ADEQUACY OF SPACE

Public Areas
   Circulation area
   Reference area
   Public catalog area
   Display areas
   Information areas
   AV use areas
   Computer area
   Book stack areas
   Reading areas
   Children's area
   Storytelling area
   Small conference rooms
   Multi-use auditorium
   Refreshment area
Staff Areas
   Office space
   Work space
   Conference space
   Storage area
   Staff break area
   Book sorting area

Source: Vance Associates

Here is another brainstorming activity. Sit down with your board and ask, "What would we do if we had $500,000 (or some other amount two or three times your current budget) to spend every year for the next ten years?" This is putting-a-man-on-the-moon kind of thinking. Look at the answers. You will probably find several great ideas that will catch the imagination of donors. Taken one at a time, these could be the target of your fundraising effort.

Do you simply need more money to run your library? Take a look at all the options and devise a plan to get it. A good first step is a five-year plan for the library that includes a fundraising component. Funding agencies, including government officials, will be impressed that you have made the effort to develop a long-range plan. They will believe that you are serious about the future of the library and will be more inclined to fund your projects. Another good book on planning is *Planning and Role Setting for Public Libraries: A Manual of Options and Procedures*, prepared for the Public Library Development Project, by Charles R. McClure *et al.* It has lots of work forms, checklists, and charts to help you plan for your library.

Next you set a target. Ask questions like: Where would we like to be? What level of improvement do we want? Can we get there ourselves? If so, when and who will be involved? Do we need help? If so, from whom? Can we measure our desired result?

These are the questions we answered when we talked about goal setting. If the roof leaks, let's fix it. But how do we eliminate the physical barriers for those who are limited by them? Is it best to start over from scratch with a new building? Or is it better to work with the existing situation? The key to this part of your planning effort is to create a specific, measurable goal with a date for accomplishment. For example, "Install carpet in the children's department by September 1."

Third is to analyze the forces at work in your community. What are the restraining forces? Anything that acts to impede the desired change is a restraining force. Anything that acts to move the change closer to its completion is a driving force. Consider restraining and driving forces. Then you can begin to deal with them in a way that will help you reach your goal.

Let's suppose that the mayor is more concerned about parks and recreation than she is about the library. Every effort to increase the library's budget is met by a salvo from the mayor that includes more favorable treatment for the park or the swimming pool. This is clearly a restraining force.

A driving force might be the president of the Friends group who gave $1,000 to the library last month. How can you capitalize on a driving force like this one? Or how can you turn a restraining force into a driving force? A conversation over lunch might be the starting point for both situations. You want to find out the motivation behind each behavior and develop strategies to turn them into a positive outcome. Brainstorming is the key to the strategy. I like to make two lists. On one side of the page I make a list of those key individuals, special groups, or audiences who use the library. On the other side I make a list of all those people who, in one way or another, control the resources of the library. How do the lists match? If they coincide, I probably have good support from the community. If not, I look for ways to change it.

TWO LISTS

Two Lists

People Who Use the Library	People Who Control Library Resources
_____	_____
_____	_____
_____	_____
_____	_____
_____	_____
_____	_____
_____	_____
_____	_____
_____	_____
_____	_____
_____	_____

The strategy is to do something that will make the lists identical— or at least add those on the second list to the first list. It may be as simple as calling the mayor's husband and asking him what kind of books the mayor likes to read. The next time you have a new book on her favorite subject, take it to her office and lend it to her. Call back in a week or so. Ask how she liked the book and offer to find another one for her. Even though your efforts might be transparent, if you are sincere, your genuine helpfulness will make a positive impression.

Once you have moved the mayor to the first list, try the city administrator or members of the city council. All people respond to attention and a genuine offer to help.

Driving and restraining forces aren't always people. Sometimes they are social structures, traditions, management, union attitudes, machines, or methods. All of these can work for you or against you. Your job is to identify the forces at work on your project and channel them to your advantage.

The fourth step is to identify possible actions and rank them by priority. For each possible action ask the following questions and limit your answers to those offered here:

1. Can we, as a group, control the events?
   A. Yes, completely.
   B. Yes, but we will need some help.
   C. No.

2. How big will the impact be?
   A. A major step forward.
   B. Moderate step forward.
   C. Minor step forward.

The answers to these two questions can help you decide whether or not to proceed with a project. Let's take an example. Suppose you want to raise $300,000 to build a new library. The action you are considering is a bond election. Ask yourself this question: Can we as a group control the events of a bond election? If the answer is: "Yes, with help" or "No" then ask: What will be the scope of the the effect? Will it be a major step forward? If you have a good chance for success, go for it.

If the result would be a minor step forward and your group cannot control the situation, forget it. Move on to an action that has a better chance for success. If, however, your group could control the event completely and it would be a major step forward, go for it. What are you waiting for? Do it today!

This is the way to rank you actions:

1-A; 2-B (Group controls event; moderate step forward).
1-B; 2-A (Group needs help; major step forward).
1-B; 2-B (Group needs help; moderate step forward).

PROJECT ACTION FORM
The following form will help you organize your work. Use one sheet for each action idea.

Project Name:

What do you want to do? Be very specific.

What are the driving forces? Who or what is working for you?

How will you put these forces to work for your project?

What are the restraining forces? Who or what can work against you to keep you from reaching your objective?

What can be done to deal with the restraining forces?

Who will be the key person in charge of this project?
Write the name here:

Who are the others who must be involved? Write their names here:

When will this project begin?

When will it end?

When this project has ended, what will the results look like? (Describe the project successfully completed).

If your group controls the action, even though it is a moderate step forward, it should become a priority because your chance of success is very high. If you have to rely on the help of others, your success is not guaranteed. Let's suppose you want to raise $3,000 for a public access computer. One fundraising option is a book sale; another is asking businesses for donations. You have had a book sale every year for the past ten years and you usually make $500 to $1,000. You have rarely asked businesses for anything more than a few gifts for prizes. It is better to make a big push for more donated books, increase your prices on your books, and promote the book sale as a fundraiser for a public access computer. Then follow up with your business solicitation for the remaining money you need. Once business people feel you are doing all you can to raise money in other ways, they will be more willing to help you.

When your brainstorming session is over and you have developed a list of ideas you think are worth trying, put each idea through the test of the two questions: 1) Can we as a group control the events? 2) How big will the impact of this action be? Make a list of action ideas and start to work on your first one.

Before you get too involved, develop action steps for each of the projects you plan. Use the brainstorming model to help you complete a Project Action Form.

The fifth step is to decide on the actions to be taken and in what order they will be taken. After completing a Project Action Form for each idea, you can arrange them according to starting date. Some actions may depend on others, so they have to be done first. For example: If you want to close the street in front of the library for a craft fair, you need city council approval before you can move ahead with your planning. Your project plan has to include the names of the person in charge and of those who will be called upon to help. In this case, each board member may be called on to contact a council member before making the formal presentation.

The sixth step is evaluation. No project is ever complete until the evaluation is done. Establish the evaluation criteria beforehand. Ask yourself, "How will I know if it works?" and "When will I know?" This helps to fix the vision mentioned earlier in this chapter.

Two questions frequently asked are: "What went well?" and "What could we do differently to make it more successful next time?" Indeed, this was the way NASA finally put a man on the moon. They learned from every Apollo mission—even the ill-fated Apollo XIII mission. Planning helps us to learn from every experience—even the ones we consider failures. Creating the strategic vision turns the process over to our subconscious, which in turn brings people, things, and ideas to us that will help us reach our goal.

SUMMARY

Some South American Indians believe in the use of hallucinogens to enable them to see into the future. They believe they can then soar with an eagle and, through its eyes, see into the future. Wouldn't it be great if we had such power. The truth is: we do. We create our own future by envisioning it first and then setting the course to make it happen.

President Kennedy set the vision for our space program, and NASA carried it out. Martin Luther King, Jr. was another visionary of our time. His "I have a dream," speech made on August 28, 1963, set the vision for the future of the civil rights movement in America. He outlined his dream for the future of the United States when all people will live and work together in peace and be judged by their character, not by the color of their skin.

Sometimes our libraries require such visionary people. Are you that person for your library? What is your vision for your library? Are you the one who will stand up and say, "I have a dream for our library."? Can you *see* what it will be like when your dream is realized?

Remember! Every good plan starts with a vision. Whether it is putting a man on the moon or making a rest room accessible to the handicapped, it starts in the mind of the person who dares to put it down on paper. Whether you are the President of the United States or a library trustee, you can make a difference. You start by writing your vision down and then sharing it with others.

5 PERFORMANCE PRECEDES FUNDING

Don Sager, Director of the Milwaukee Public Library makes these suggestions as a preface to any fundraising effort:

1. Have your act together first.
2. Take a look at your situation.
3. Ask yourself, "How could we do better?"
4. Toot your own horn long and loud and often.

When people give money to libraries they want their gift to make a difference. They don't want it to be used to make up for the benign neglect of a governing body. The job of all library managers is to make sure that their libraries perform well—that people get what they want when they go there. This chapter is about enhancing the image and the performance of the library.

Public Relations

In my article "New Visibility for the Small PL," (*Wilson Library Bulletin*, January 1977), I pointed out that all libraries have public relations. Whether they like or not—whether it's good or bad, high-powered or low-key—all libraries have it. Unfortunately, for the small public library it is often low-profile and seldom pushed beyond the cloistered walls of the library itself.

When I first moved to South Carolina in 1971, I thought I would impress people by identifying myself as the *director* of the county library. A common response was, "Oh, that's nice. Where is the library?" I soon realized that the library needed me more than I needed the library. Even though it was located in the heart of the retail district, the library was so low-key that most people didn't know where it was.

I had to increase visibility for the library, but before I could do that, I had to produce the programs people expected from a public library. It doesn't pay to advertise if you don't have the goods to back your advertising. I could have traveled all over the county inviting people to come to the library, but they would never have returned if we didn't have what they needed when they came.

It was no surprise that the library needed money. We had less than $1 per capita for library services—barely enough to hire a few staff members and buy very few books, with no money for public relations. Fundraising was in order.

As I mentioned back in the introduction, my first fundraising opportunity came because we needed money to promote the library. So I prepared a small project and asked a bank to underwrite it. I asked the bank president for $300 to pay for a library publicity booklet published by Channing-Bete. Information about the library and the bank's logo would be printed on the back. She agreed to the project, and we were on our way.

With a booklet in hand for each student, I went to every elementary school in the county. I presented a program, passed out the booklets, and gave every child an application form for a library card. We mailed library cards to the children with a letter encouraging them to use the library. We also offered a card to their parents.

Borrower registration doubled overnight, and circulation increased dramatically. When parents and children discovered their library, funding started to improve. When people believe you are doing something that will benefit them, they will see that you get the money you need to do even more for them.

Burnishing the library's image

Sometimes our problem is not our performance, but our image. We are doing a good job, but nobody knows it. That's why we have to take time to see ourselves as others see us. The clerk at the supermarket who responded with, "Oh, where is the library?" gave me an outsider's window through which I could see the library.

If the image of your library is incorrect, you have to get outside the library to fix it. Changing public perception without getting out of the library is like taking a bath in a wet suit. You never get to the heart of the problem. You become so accustomed to the way you see your situation that you can't see it the way others do.

You could have all kinds of videos, CD's, and the latest bestsellers, but if people think of your library as a warehouse of books, and the librarian as their baby-sitter, you will always have funding problems.

Stop!

Take a minute right now to assess your library's image. How do people see it? How do you see it? Make a list of three things you could do next week that would make a difference in how the public sees your library. Write one of the ideas on your "To-Do List" for next Monday.

Then do it.

GETTING STARTED

Did you have trouble thinking of some ideas to enhance your library's image? Here are a few you might try:

1. Create a one-page, three-fold library brochure. Include library services, special programs for special groups, hours, address, telephone number, names of staff and board members. You can do this with a typewriter. Use a photocopier to duplicate it. It doesn't take much money to do an attractive brochure. If you want to get fancy, a desktop publisher can put it together in a few hours.
2. Take a stack of your newly created brochures around to the business people in town. Tell them you are promoting the services of the library. Offer help to find information for their business. Ask for suggestions to make the library more visible in the community.
3. Have business cards printed for the librarian and all board members, with individual names plus the library's name, address and telephone number on one side and the library hours on the other.
4. Take the head of the Chamber of Commerce to lunch. Ask for ideas to improve the library's image with the business community.
5. Obtain a list of local service groups and clubs. They are always looking for programs; offer to do one for them.

Did you notice that all of these suggestions require that you get out of the library and do something? Targeting public relations activities to those who already come to the library is like preaching to the choir. They already know and love the library. You want to reach those who don't know your library, but are ready to be converted.

You may want someone from outside your organization to help you get started or be a sounding board for your ideas. "A big advantage of hiring a professional," says Tom Vance of Kenneth M. Vance Associates (professional fundraising consultants), "is they can provide you with a clearer assessment of your potential." They can tell you if you need to build your image or sharpen your performance before you ask people to support a fundraising effort.

CHECKING PERFORMANCE

Now take a look at your actual performance. Do your hours meet the needs of the community? Do you have the materials to give the people what they want when they come in? What about the staff? Are they friendly, helpful, and well-trained? What do you do if the library doesn't have the material requested? How well is your library performing? How are you perceived by the people in your community? Take the test, Checklist for Library Image and Performance to see how well you are doing.

Thomas Childers and Nancy Van House in their *Public Library Effectiveness Study,* found that various groups considered the following to be important when assessing public library effectiveness:

- Convenience of hours
- Staff helpfulness
- Range of services
- Range of materials
- Services suited to community needs
- Materials quality
- Staff quality
- Materials availability
- Convenience of location
- Contribution to community well-being
- Managerial competence
- Awareness of service.

They surveyed community leaders, local officials, friends, trustees, users, library managers, and service librarians. The unusual finding of their survey was that all groups tended to respond alike.

The findings of this research point us toward more effective library service if we will evaluate our performance according to the criteria and make changes to meet the needs of the community.

Public libraries are judged on many fronts. Dr. Childers found that public library effectiveness is defined by many attributes. All 61 of the items listed in the survey were perceived as important measures of library effectiveness.

If we take the concept of convenience of hours and put it through a planning model, we will develop a good plan for making our hours more convenient. We start by asking ourselves:

Where are we now? (Are our hours convenient for most people?)

Where would we like to be? (Do we want more hours? Or to change the ones we have?)

What is our goal? (Do we want to be open five nights per week and all day Saturday and Sunday?)

What are the driving and restraining forces? Money has to be one. (What will help us reach this goal? What will keep us from it?)

What actions do we want to take?

CHECKLIST FOR LIBRARY IMAGE AND PERFORMANCE

	Yes	No	Suggested Action
1. Is the name of your library clearly visible from the street?	___	___	_____
2. Are library hours posted so they can be read by someone from the street?	___	___	_____
3. Is library parking adequate?	___	___	_____
4. Is library parking specially marked for short-term parking? For the handicapped?	___	___	_____
5. Does the library have a curb-side book deposit for after-hours book return?	___	___	_____
6. Do library grounds and exterior appearance meet or exceed community standards?	___	___	_____
7. Is the library accessible to the handicapped?	___	___	_____
8. Are library hours adequate to meet community needs?	___	___	_____
9. Is the library collection current and readily available?	___	___	_____
10. Do the books look new and inviting to the reader?	___	___	_____
11. Does the physical arrangement draw people in?	___	___	_____
12. Is the staff friendly and courteous?	___	___	_____
13. Is the staff knowledgeable and helpful?	___	___	_____
14. Is the library a nice place to be?	___	___	_____

Can we control the events ourselves? Will they make a big difference?

What will we actually do?

Who will be responsible?

When will we start?

When will we end?

What will the successful change look like?

When and how will we know we have completed it?

You can improve the performance of your library in other areas if you will take the time to study what you are doing and make plans to enhance your service.

SEEKING MORE TAX MONEY

A wonderful side benefit of fundraising is the positive impact you create for tax initiatives. A good fundraising effort will spotlight your need and enhance your chances for increased tax support.

Early in 1988 the Great Bend Public Library solicited cash gifts through a letter explaining our dire financial circumstance. We raised over $3,000, and this effort focused the voters on our need. A few months later, when we asked them to approve a mill levy increase for the library, they did.

There is little or no difference between selling people on the idea of giving money to the library and raising taxes to support the library. Karen Givens, Librarian of South New Berlin Free Library said, "Our success story involved petitioning the taxpayers in the school district to allow for additional taxes to go toward supporting the operation of the library. Since that measure was whole-heartedly endorsed by the people, we have not needed to do additional fundraising."

Robert Hartsook suggests establishing your identity by answering the question: Who are we? He says, "Keep your image simple. Externalize your program. Describe it the way the donor sees it. Be consistent and persistent. Do it the same over and over again. Be prepared to explain it one more time."

Performance does precede funding. They sustain each other. A library that does not give the people what they want cannot expect the support it needs. A poorly funded library cannot give the people what they want. If people perceive libraries to be effective, funding will follow.

SUMMARY

Do people get what they want when they come to your library? If so, you will probably have the support you need to get the funding you need. Sometimes we have to see ourselves through the eyes of others to become aware of our shortcomings. The self-assessment tests in this chapter will help you see your library more clearly.

6 INCREASING TAX DOLLARS

The best place to raise money for your library is at the ballot box or at city hall. If people can give your library more tax money by voting for it, you have the best way to raise more money for your library—taxes. First of all, it is renewable with little or no effort. Except in a few states, once taxes for library operation are on the books, they stay on the books. You don't have to go out and raise the same amount of money next year. Street fairs and book sales may be a lot of fun, but they can get stale and your volunteers may get tired. So, when it comes to fundraising, look first to the voters. Over time, it is the most effective way to raise money.

The mayor of Ida, Illinois, (population 15,176) was a helpful member of the Friends. With his assistance, the Friends wrapped a blue ribbon made of crepe paper around the entire library building to publicize the election. They also wrapped blue ribbons around trees on city property all around the town to remind people to support the library. Not all of this was fundraising exactly, but it was part of the overall program. Newspapers and television from the neighboring large city of Rockford, Illinois, covered the event. The referendum passed by 72 percent.

Are you getting your fair share?

Are you authorized to levy five mills and are only levying four? Why? What would it take to levy the full amount? Although the public is generally against tax increases, in my experience a majority of people will vote in favor of giving the library more money, even if it means higher taxes. In 1988 the people of Great Bend, Kansas voted for a mill levy increase for the library in the face of a bad economy. Withholding your request for additional taxes because of a bad economy will not help economic conditions.

If you can't go for a referendum and your city commission has absolute control over your budget you may have to resort to some gentle arm twisting. Even if your library is doing a good job and you have the support of the people, you may have to resort to other measures.

Try asking a few influential friends to contact the city officials. My doctor in South Carolina asked the chairman of the County Council why he didn't give the library more money. He said he would if he could, but he didn't have the support of the other council members.

Libraries that have access to an initiative petition can push for a referendum. For example: If ten percent of the voters sign a petition to vote for a tax increase for the library, it has to be put on

PUBLISHED DATA.

Most state libraries publish public annual statistics reports. You can get a sense of how your library compares with others by comparing your numbers with the numbers of libraries more or less your size.

the ballot. People will support a library that gives them what they want.

Sometimes statistical data can help you convince the city council to give the library more money. Compare the tax dollars received by the library for the past ten years to the total budget of the city for the same years. Express the library's income as a percentage of the total municipal budget. Plot this information on a line graph. Show the municipal budget and the library income from the city in dollars. Insert the library's percentage for each year. If the library's percentage decreases over time, you have justified an increase.

The year I won the largest increase in South Carolina was the year I used statistics to show that the the library's portion of county revenue had decreased over the years. The night of the budget hearing I had charts and graphs taped all over the walls of the council's chamber. It may have looked funny, but it worked.

Caution!

If the statistics don't support your viewpoint, you obviously need more statistics. You must be doing something right, if the library has increased its share of the city budget over time! Figure out how it happened and keep it up. Who can argue with success?

If you have enough statistics, you can prove anything. Gather data about library usage. Circulation, reference questions, story hour participation, registered borrowers, etc., all used together can build a strong case for increased funding.

TYPES OF APPEAL TO SUPPORT A BUDGET REQUEST

Authority: State Aid requirement. If we are to continue to receive state aid, state law says that tax revenue for the library cannot be reduced.

Pride Committee: The Kansas Pride Committee has established $4,500 as the minimum local revenue for the library to be eligible for Pride Recognition.

Example: Another library our size, the new McCracken Library, cost $60,000. We could do the same.

Comparison: Compare your library to a relevant standard. State standards for a library our size, call for 25 periodical subscriptions. We have ten subscriptions. In 1980 the library received 5.1 percent of the city's tax revenue. Today it receives 4.6 percent.

Identity: Something valued by members of the city commission. If they have demonstrated a desire to provide for children and youth, emphasize the value of the library's story hour. If they have done a lot for recreation, point out the library's sports collection or the videos.

Experts: Select libraries specialists who are far enough away to be recognized as authorities. The State Librarian says that we should be spending 60 percent of our budget on salaries and benefits.

Individualize: Specific benefit to the city officials. The library is an information place for city offices, the mayor and council members. We will be able to keep the library open more hours. Helping the library will make friends in the community.

Sense of Fairness: Uniform salaries. Is it right for comparable workers in city government to earn $7 per hour, when library employes earn only $5?

Community Pride: The library is a source of pride for the whole community. Let's keep it a place of beauty and a symbol of our city's dedication to progress.

Try using the following planning sheets to help plan for your next budget presentation.

PREPARING THE BUDGET REQUEST.

Prepare well in advance of your appearance before the governing body. Think of everything you can to help your cause. Try to figure out everything someone might say to argue against your presentation. Try to think the way the council members will think. Envision your presentation from their viewpoint. Then envision yourself standing up in front of the council and making a flawless speech. Rehearse it again and again in your mind. This will strengthen your position.

First, establish the library as a viable, valuable service organization. Try any or all of the following arguments:

- (number) percent of the people in our town who have a library card.
- Last year we circulated (number) volumes.
- This is equal to (number) books circulated per capita.
- The president of the chamber of commerce said, "We have the best library in the state."

- No other agency in town does what the library does.
- In a survey we did last year, (number) percent of the people said they got what they wanted when they came to the library.
- The library meets the knowledge, information, and reading needs of the people.
- Interlibrary loan expands the resources for our patrons.
- We meet the special needs of shut-ins through our home delivery service.
- The library saves people money. For every book they can get at the library free and don't have to buy, they save about $20.

This is your time to brag about your library. Do it. You are showing confidence and commitment—not conceit. Think of as many positive things to say about your library as you can.

The next step is to use the budget and existing conditions to illustrate your library's need. Start by analyzing the budget and determine the library's priorities. Use only the data which will present the library's need. Be specific yet brief in describing the situation. Know exactly what you want. Make a specific request. Ask for a dollar amount. Be silent. Wait for questions.

INCREASING STATE AID

If state aid in your state is low or nonexistent, organize the public libraries and lobby the state legislature. Public libraries are a statewide resource and deserve statewide funding. Here are a few lobbying suggestions:

- Learn the legislative process in your state and teach it to others.
- Organize the library community in a way that involves the state library, but only as an information gathering and dissemination unit.
- Generate groundswell support by involving every public library, their boards, and their patrons.
- Sponsor legislative receptions in the library. Invite local legislators and their constituents.
- Encourage the state library association to sponsor legislative workshops.
- Persuade the state library association to develop a legislative agenda.
- Develop your legislative strategy through a legislative committee.

- Make sure that the committee is composed of librarians affiliated with both political parties.
- Know the issues yourself and make sure others do too.
- Hold "Library Legislative Day" at the capitol during the legislative session.
- Learn how to communicate with your legislators using letters, telephone calls, and personal visits.
- Stay abreast of pending legislation as it works its way through the legislative process.
- Make timely contacts with your legislators.

RULES FOR WRITING TO LEGISLATORS

Be brief. Keep your letter to a half page, if possible, and never more than one page. You may include a fact sheet if you want to, but don't count on it being read. Put all the important stuff in your letter.

Be specific. Identify the piece of legislation you are concerned about, by bill number if possible.

State your position. They need to know how you feel.

Explain the benefits. Tell how their constituents will benefit if they vote they way you want them to.

Urge their support. Ask them to vote on the measure in support of your position.

Ask for a response. You are asking them to commit to a position and let you know how they intend to vote.

Close. Offer to provide additional information if they need it. Sign your name and mail it.

A letter from the librarian is important, but a letter from your board members and patrons will have an even greater impact. It may take special encouragement. Try giving them this information and drafting a sample letter. Urge them to put the ideas into their own words. Identical letters to one legislator from several people lessen the value of all letters.

Handwritten letters from individuals have the most influence of all. They are the letters the legislator reads first. Librarians and board members can be perceived as self-serving advocates of library programs. Librarians are also seen as the local experts on

SAMPLE LETTER
Here is a sample letter written to a legislator in support of increased state-aid to libraries.

Happy Valley Public Library
111 North Main Street
Happy Valley, Kansas 66645

March 23, 1990

Representative Bill Williams
123 State Capitol Building
Topeka, Kansas 66612

Dear Representative Williams:

House Bill 2345 provides $555,000 in matching funds to help libraries buy computers. Your support of this bill will help every library in Kansas tap into the excellent computerized telecommunications network available to Kansas libraries. No matter where they live, people will be able to get what they want when they go to their library because their library will be part of an automated interlibrary system. This is a statewide resource and should be accessible to all.

Please vote in favor of House Bill 2345.

I look forward to hearing your position this issue.

Sincerely,

Librarian

---

library matters. Individuals have nothing to gain except better service from their library.

Just as fundraising is selling, so is legislative lobbying. You are trying to persuade a group of legislators that more money for state aid to public libraries will benefit them, their constituents, and the state. Don't give up on the first try. It usually take two or three years, maybe more, to get a new piece of legislation through the process. Legislators have to understand that you are serious about your proposal. Your persistence is one way of telling them.

Counties, townships, or other entities outside your taxing district may be willing to appropriate money for your library if they perceive a benefit to their constituents for which no taxes are being levied. For your presentation to them, follow the same pattern suggested earlier in this chapter. Focus on the number of borrowers your library serves who live in the tax district you are addressing.

SUMMARY

Tax dollars are the best way to fund your library. They are steady and they come in every year without soliciting donors. If you aren't getting your share, spend some time with your board to develop ways of making a case for more money. If you need more money than you can reasonably expect from tax sources, the next chapters suggest how to solicit it from willing donors.

PLANNING A BUDGET REQUEST

1. What arguments (justifications) will you use?

2. What statistics will you use?

3. Do they support your argument?

4. What will be the format of your presentation? (Written only Will you have a chance to speak?)

5. Is your proposal clearly written and easy to understand?

6. Do your charts, graphs, etc. support your arguments?

7. Is everything neatly done and easy to understand?

8. Who will make the presentation? (Who has the most clout with the City Council?)

9. How will you pre-test your presentation? (Try it on friends or co-workers?)

10. How will you handle questions?

11. Who do you have lined up to lobby the governing body in support of your budget?

STATISTICS FOR BUDGET PRESENTATION

1. What is the city population?

2. How many registered borrowers does the library have?

3. What percent of city residents have library cards?

4. How many borrowers live outside the library district?

5. How many books does your library have?

6. How many books per capita?

7. How does this compare to other libraries of your size in the state?

8. How many hours per week is your library open?

9. How does this compare to other similar sized libraries?

10. What was last year's circulation?

11. What was the circulation total before that?

12. What was the circulation five years ago?

13. How many circulations per capita last year?

14. How many each year for the past five years?

15. How does this compare with other libraries in your area?

16. What is your library's total budget?

17. What percent comes from the city?

18. What percent comes from the county?

19. What percent comes from the state?

20. What percent comes from other sources?

21. How do these figures compare with statewide averages?

22. How much money did you spend on books last year?

23. What percent was that?

24. How much on salaries?

25. What percent was that?

26. How much on operations?

27. What percent was that?

28. How do these figures compare to other libraries in your area?

    Books and materials: Higher, lower, or the same?

    Salaries: Higher, lower, or the same?

    Operations: Higher, lower, or the same?

27. What three things does your library need most?

28. How does the public feel about these needs?

29. What priority does the library have with the city commission?

30. Which board members have the most influence with the city commission?

7 SOLICITING DONATIONS

"The best way to get on in the world is to make people believe it's to their advantage to help you."

Jean de La Bruijére

The most effective way to raise money from private sources is to ask individuals for it. If they think it is to their advantage to give you money, so much the better. It is not as hard as you think. The following, in priority order, are the most effective ways of asking people to donate to your organization:

1. Friend to friend, face to face
2. Peer to peer, face to face
3. Non-peer to someone higher, face to face
4. Stranger to stranger, face to face
5. Friend to friend, peer to peer, etc. on the telephone
6. Telephone call preceded by mail solicitation
7. Telephone
8. Personal handwritten letter, direct mail
9. Personalized (Dear Barbara and George) typed letter, direct mail
10. Impersonal (Dear Friend, Resident) direct mail
11. Paid advertising on television
12. Paid advertising on radio
13. Paid advertising in newspaper

The best prospects to contact can be ranked in the following order:

1. Those who have already given major gifts to your library
2. Those who have made regular donations to the library
3. Those who have given only once to the library
4. Library board members
5. Friends of the library
6. People who have paid to attend a special event at the library
7. Those who have donated books to the library
8. Library volunteers
9. Regular library patrons
10. Members of the city council

11. Registered borrowers of the library
12. The general public—older people first

MOTIVATING DONORS

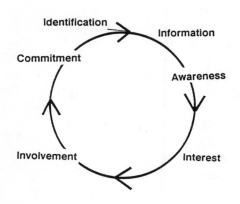

Evaluate prospective donors on their capacity to give and their interest in your organization. You may know someone who has millions of dollars to give away but has little interest in your library. On the other hand, you probably know lots of people who are very interested in the library but have little money to give. The fundraiser's job, then, is to find those people who have a high interest in the organization and have plenty of money to give, and then to ask them for it.

Since you probably don't have a long line of interested rich people, your task is to turn the general public into prospective donors. Then you have to convert prospective donors to active donors and active donors into major contributors. David Dunlop, an educational fundraising consultant, has developed what he calls the "moves model." It is a planned program designed to make people aware of your organization and "moving" them toward a gift. Your research may uncover some hot prospects with lots of money, but not all of them will feel the same way you do about your library. They may not even know you exist or have a need. So once you have found people with money, your job is to move them from a lack of awareness about your cause to the point of making a donation.

You start them on a diet of information about the library. A newsletter is a good tool to create awareness. It focuses on the individual and the library. It may take several contacts before the prospects becomes aware of the library's need. The next step is to involve them in a library activity, preferably not connected with fundraising. Just invite them to a program—brown-bag book reviews or a puppet show or an art reception—anything to get them into the library. The next step is to involve the individuals in the library in a way that makes them aware of the library's financial need.

The right person is someone with the amount of money you need and a desire to give it to the library. They generally don't walk in off the street and write a check to the library. Usually, you have to find them, cultivate them, and win them over to the point of giving. This is the essence of fundraising.

USING BUTTONS

My fundraising friend at Kansas State University, Thomas Parish, uses buttons to get other people to ask him about his fundraising effort. He uses slogans like:

"Teaching future educators is more than a life-long process."
"Is education important? Then put your money where your mouth is."
"Helping students learn can be more than the pursuit of a lifetime."

Dr. Parish says, "When you ask about something, you are committed to sit and listen. If you have asked and listened, and you can't reject the major premise, you have to buy." This brand of passive fundraising helps you select your potential donors. When you talk to those who ask you about your button, you have pre-selected those with a better-than-average chance of giving. Not only that, but you have psychologically set them up to listen to you. They are obliged to listen until you stop talking. They may turn you off emotionally after the first five seconds, but at least you had a chance to tell your story one more time.

Parish says, "A button is a silent salesman. You want people to ask you about your button. It is a matter of opportunity and education. Never worry about whether you have a good opportunity. Just be sure to be good to every opportunity."

CAPITAL FUND DRIVE

A capital fund drive is the most effective way to raise money in a relatively short period of time. You raise more and spend less than in any other fundraising activity. You conduct a capital fund drive to build a new library or create an endowment.

The best thing about a capital fund drive is there is a beginning and an end, usually close together. You are asking people to give over a three- to five-year period. They know and you know that you are not going to ask again for the same project.

You recruit volunteers to do the asking for gifts. One of them should be an individual with connections and influence—someone who can bring people into the group and then go out and get money too.

You start with a clear vision of your project. This can be an architectural drawing. A benefactor in Ellsworth, Kansas, thought so much of the library's project that he spent several hundred dollars for a scale model of the new library. It is easier to get people to give if they can see what they are giving to.

FEASIBILITY STUDY

If you have a project that will cost $300,000 or more, hire a professional fundraising consultant to conduct a feasibility study first. Don't "pass go" without it. A feasibility study gets the process started. Some library board members become immobilized by the enormity of the fundraising goal. The feasibility study moves them from a passive to an active role—nudging their involvement.

PREPARING A CASE STATEMENT

About the time you are conducting the feasibility study, begin preparing your case statement. Some professionals like to take a one-page draft of the document with them when they visit with the community leaders. A case statement is a brief summary of your library's purpose, the need for the fundraising project, and how you plan to accomplish your objective.

First, state the mission of your library. Do it in 25 words or less—and make it in terms of benefits to the customer. Some library mission statements go on for a page or more and usually get bogged down in library jargon like bibliographic access, collection development, and maintaining a viable collection of materials of various formats. Why not say:

> "The business of the library is to meet the information, knowledge and reading needs of the people?"

Try to see the library as your customers do. They don't care about form or format. They want information. They want a book to read. How the library accomplishes its mission of providing information knowledge and reading to its customers is not part of the mission statement.

Once you have developed your short mission statement, you need to make a brief statement about your project. In *Megatrends,* John Naisbitt said, "Strategic planning is worthless unless there is first a strategic vision." You are creating a strategic vision when you say, "We want to build a new library." You flesh out the vision when you describe its shape and dimensions. It becomes more real when you draw a picture of it and give it a name. Some libraries have given their project a name to generate more interest—even to humanize it. NASA named the missions to the moon Apollo I,

Apollo II, and so on. Everyone knew what Apollo stood for and everyone felt a part of lunar exploration.

One of the libraries in the survey had a Pete the Penny campaign as a fundraiser. Children collected 100 pennies and brought them to the library. The people in Rhinelander, Wisconsin, caught the vision of thousands of pennies marching into the library—going to work to remodel the library.

After you describe your project and give it a character, tell how you are going to accomplish the task. If you have a big project with many different fundraising activities, outline each project and the anticipated income from each.

Set a goal. And remember: Write it down! There is tremendous power in creating a vision. If you can write it down you can have it.

SELECTING THE CHAIR

Part of the consultant's job in the feasibility study is to help select the chair of the capital campaign committee. Although I strongly recommend that you hire a professional consultant, it is certainly possible for you to do a feasibility study yourself. Don't be too quick to jump into the task, though. The information you gather from visits with community leaders won't be as accurate. They will tell you what they think you want to hear.

There are no perfect formulas for selecting the chair of your capital campaign. However, it should be someone capable of making a major gift—one of the top five. Otherwise, other large gifts will not come in.

Use the Chair Selection Worksheet and the Chair Selection Matrix (pages 94-95) to help evaluate each candidate. The matrix is also useful for many other fundraising decisions or problem-solving situations. Start by creating a list of possible solutions. Write those across the top of the page. Then develop the criteria for a good solution by listing characteristics you would like to see in the ideal solution. Test each possible solution against the criteria. The best solution will have the most check marks.

Here is how the matrix works. Some criteria might be:

- Committed to the project.
- Ability to make a significant gift.
- Ability to ask for the lead gift.
- Enthusiasm for library fundraising.
- Knowledge of library's fundraising project.
- A friend to everyone in town.
- Personal influence (clout).

- Ability to attract and recruit committee members.
- Ability to delegate effectively.
- Broad minded.
- Confident.
- Optimistic about the committee's success.

Next you write the names at the top of the list. In a small community, you may have only three names. It is better to have

COMMITTEE CHAIR

SELECTION MATRIX

Criteria	Names								

CHAIR SELECTION WORKSHEET

Name: (Fill out a worksheet for each person to be considered.)

POINT SYSTEM:

5 points = highest mark, the best.

3 points = good, but leaves something to be desired.

1 point = clearly not strong in this area.

1. Is this person capable of making a major gift to our project?
Comment:

2. Does this person appreciate and use the library on a regular basis?
Comment:

3. Will this person make a big gift to our project?
Comment:

4. Does this person have the personal clout to get the big bucks for our project?
Comment:

5. Can this person secure a lead gift of 10 percent of our goal?
Comment:

6. Can this person recruit others who will give themselves and solicit the money we need?
Comment:

7. Can this person train and motivate others to solicit?
Comment:

8. Can this person delegate and follow-through?
Comment:

9. What is this person's track-record for other fundraising projects?
Comment:

10. Will this person's name associated with our fund drive help us?
Comment:

Chart of Giving

Campaign Goal= $250,000

	Number	Amount	Percent	Names
Lead gift	1	$25,000	10%	_____
				_____
				_____
Lead gifts	2	$12,500	10%	_____
				_____
				_____
				_____
				_____
Major gifts	5	$5,000	10%	_____
				_____
				_____
				_____
				_____
				_____
				_____
				_____
Big gifts	10	$2,500	10%	_____
				_____
				_____
				_____
				_____
				_____
				_____
				_____
				_____
				_____

more if you can. Next mark a check by each name for each criteria, if that person is strong in that area. It is absolutely essential that the chair of the committee be willing and able to make a significant gift. You will find that the value of other top gifts will cluster around the gift made by the chair of the committee. This process of selecting the chair of the fundraising committee should be conducted by the group ultimately responsible for the welfare of the library. If no one feels good about the choice, review the process. Listen to your feelings.

You will want to interview everyone you are considering for committee chair. Write out a job description for the committee chair. Write across it draft copy. Take this document with you when you visit the few people you have selected as possible candidates for the job. Ask each one what they think of the draft document. Ask them if they can think of anything you left out or should have included. You can also take a draft copy of your case statement and the chart of giving. Their reactions to the questions will be very revealing. The people you visit will begin to internalize the purpose of your visit. They will see themselves in the role of committee chair, without your asking. They will begin to think of their own contribution to the fund drive. You will be surprised at the answers you get.

Robert Hartsook recommends a chart of giving that looks like the one on the following page. It represents the top end of the giving scale. He believes that the goal is possible if the fundraising group can confidently write down three names for each gift sought. Some donors will not give at the anticipated level, but will give at a lower level.

CHAIRING THE FUNDRAISING COMMITTEE
What does it mean to be the chair of the Fundraising Committee? It means that you will have to take charge in a way that will raise the money the library needs to complete its project.

The Chair of the Capital Fund Drive Committee will be expected to:

- be absolutely committed to the project
- make a significant (sacrificial) gift
- ask for the lead gift—the single largest gift—or help someone else do it
- attract, recruit, and solicit five team leaders
- be enthusiastic about raising money for the library
- generate that same enthusiasm in others

- know everything about your library's fundraising project
- be friendly to everyone in town
- use his or her personal influence for the good of the library
- know the committee system and delegate effectively
- work with the people who may express differing opinions
- never doubt victory.

I can't overemphasize the importance of selecting the right person to be the committee chair. Helping select the chair is often the task of a professional fundraiser. If you hire a consultant, it is likely that he or she will lead you through a similar process. Whoever you select must make or secure the lead gift or one on of the top five gifts. Remember that other major gifts tend to cluster around the largest gift made by key members of the committee.

I was asked in one of my workshops how important this point is. I answered, "If you want to raise $1 million, the right to be chair of the fundraising committee may well have a pricetag of $50,000 or even $100,000." If you have someone who is willing to give $50,000 to the library, he or she will likely be willing to support that investment by becoming the driving force for your fund drive.

Joan Flanagan suggests a chart that looks like the one at right. The giving pattern will not follow the chart exactly, but it does provide a guide for the fundraising group.

Gift Size	Number Needed	Dollar Total	People to Ask
$40,000	1	$40,000	2
20,000	4	80,000	8
10,000	6	60,000	12
5,000	14	70,000	28
2,000	35	70,000	70
1,000	60	60,000	120
100	200	20,000	400

Total Goal $400,000

Once you have selected the committee chair and have a financial commitment from him or her, the next step is to select and recruit team chairs. These people must also be well-respected community leaders. The chair of the fundraising committee and someone else—perhaps the president of the library board—make a personal visit to each potential team leader and ask them for a major gift. If they say yes, ask them to help out on the committee. They will probably be willing to help. Each team leader needs to recruit and solicit five volunteers.

So far, you have recruited the committee chair and five team leaders—sometimes known as the fundraising board or steering committee. Every one of them should be expected to make a major gift and/or help secure one. Joan Flanagan says that 20 percent of the amount you need should come from this group, and that they should secure the next 20 percent, for a total of 40 percent before you publicly announce your fundraising campaign. You can reach your goal if you have 40 percent of your money in the bank before the public campaign starts.

The next step is to recruit committee workers. They are the rank and file who will go out, knock on doors, and ask people for money. The key to recruiting them is selling them on the worth of the library's project. Then give them clear instructions and the latitude to do the job as they see fit.

Be honest with them.

Give them lots of support.

Bonnie Williamson, librarian in Havre, Montana, raised over $360,000 with volunteers. She suggests, "Recruit as many reliable volunteers as you can. The few faithful ones were a tired bunch when we finally reached our goal."

VOLUNTEERS AND TEAM LEADERS

You need about one volunteer for every five people to be contacted. They should also be expected to give. People who ask others for donations without having given something themselves are less effective than those who have given.

So now you have the board and the volunteer solicitors selected, and everyone so far has given or made a pledge. What is the next step? You organize them into logical committees, perhaps the Big Gifts Committee, the Residential Committee, and the Rural Committee.

Jean Rahn, Executive Director of the Eastern Montana College Foundation, in Billings, Montana, organizes her annual fund drive committees according to the size of gift to be solicited—$1,000, $500, $250, $100, and so on. Her effective approach is to have people select the size of gift they want to solicit. The size of gift you are seeking matches your own gift. If you are seeking gifts of $1,000, you are expected to give $1,000.

The key to asking volunteer solicitors to give is: don't assume anything. If they are willing to ask others for money to support your cause, they will probably give more than you think. Think big. You will flatter them by asking them for more than you think they can give.

All along, you should be developing your prospective donor list. This could be as easy, or as hard, as going through the local telephone directory and copying every name onto a card. The secretary of the steering committee in Ellis, Kansas, wrote every name address and telephone number of everyone in the telephone directory on 3x5 cards. This is a job for staff if you have enough paid people to do it.

In a small community you want to give everyone the opportunity to own a part of the new library. You don't miss very many homes when you use the telephone directory. In a larger community going through the phone book would be impractical.

Another way to get the names of prospects is to brainstorm. The same rules apply. Don't discount any suggestions. Write down every name mentioned.

Here are a few other possibilities:

- library users
- people who have given books to the library
- people who have made memorial gifts in the past
- people who have volunteered service to the library
- share lists with the community college
- guest registers from special events at the library
- high school alumni lists
- country club list
- chamber of commerce list
- voter registration lists.

Next look up the names, addresses, and telephone numbers and make out a card for each prospect. If you are creating a long-term donor list, you will want to keep more information on the card.

You will want to keep track of:

- age
- family
- church
- work

- volunteer
- where they live (census tract)
- where they live (political precinct).

You may even want to create a full-page form similar to the one shown on page 102. On the other hand, if this is a one-shot deal and you only need money for a new library, don't go to all that trouble.

Filling one of these out for every household in town could be a big job for one person. Use volunteers or staff or a combination.

Once you have the names, addresses, and telephone numbers and all the prospects on cards or forms, it is time to do your research and rate prospects. The purpose of rating prospects is to develop a consensus about the giving potential for each prospect. Robert Hartsook suggests evaluating prospective donors on their capacity to give and their interest in your organization. You need to know this before you start asking or you could miss a potentially large gift or embarrass yourself by asking too little.

Jean Rahn handles it this way. She invites the division heads and team leaders to breakfast between 7:00 and 9:00 a.m.— keeping it very informal. They don't all come at the same time. After each has eaten, she brings a stack of prospect forms and asks the leader to project the maximum gift the prospect might be willing to give— using these categories:

- More than $1,000
- $1,000
- $500
- $250
- $100.

There is no conferring or sitting around the table asking, "How much can we expect from Harry Smith?" This is the time for making marginal notes that can help the askers: "Business has been bad for Bill this year." "I think this was the best year ever for Susan," or "John and his wife divorced last year." All of this information is confidential, of course.

After all the team leaders have rated the prospects, the executive director and the committee chair make the final rating and assign each prospect to a category by amount. At this point in the process, they pull all of the names of prospects who were rated at $500 or more and give them to the Big Gifts Committee. However you do it, prospects are assigned to teams, and the team chairs then assign them to individual solicitors.

Donor Prospect Form
Confidential

Name _____

Spouse or contact _____

Home telephone _____

Home mailing address _____

City, state zip_____

Business or employment_____

Business address _____

City, state zip _____

Business telephone _____

Personal information:

    Family_____

    Church_____

    Hobbies_____

    Talents _____

Special comments:

_____

_____

_____

Giving History:

Year	Amount	Solicitor	Suggestion for next year.
_____	_____	_____	_____
_____	_____	_____	_____
_____	_____	_____	_____
_____	_____	_____	_____
_____	_____	_____	_____
_____	_____	_____	_____
_____	_____	_____	_____

Jean Rahn invites the $1,000 team members in to suggest the names they want. Generally, peers ask peers for money. Sometimes prospects are assigned by geography, but then solicitors should be assigned to prospective donors outside their neighborhood.

Once you have assigned the prospects to the askers, invite everyone in for your kickoff breakfast and give them the names of their prospects. Have the names typed on cards or prospect forms that fit in a notebook. Give the team members copies of the case statement brochure. Give them a receipt book and whatever other material you think they need. Do it at a breakfast because the purpose of this meeting is to get everyone excited. If you have the kickoff at breakfast, the volunteers have all day to go out with enthusiasm and ask for the money. The best time to contact the people on your list is the same day you receive the list. Encourage all of your solicitors to make all of their calls that day. If you have the kickoff at night, the enthusiasm is gone by the next morning.

What do you do at a kickoff breakfast? You thank your solicitors for volunteering and praise them for their gifts. Everyone should have made a gift by now. You announce the amount of money raised so far. People like to help with an effort that is well on its way to success. They like to be part of a winning team.

Everyone should clearly understand and be committed to the purpose of the fundraiser. They should be anxious to go to work on the project. You may have all new people. Give them a tour of the library and treat them as VIPs. Instruct them on how to handle objections. Encourage them to make their calls immediately.

TRAINING VOLUNTEERS

My salesman friend Jim Keller suggests holding a meeting with everyone there. He says, "Fill them with product knowledge (What does the library do? How is it funded? What does it need?) Come up with a list of eight to ten reasons why people will donate to your cause. Brainstorming works well for this part of the meeting. Ask them why they think people will want to give to your project.

"Then come up with two or three scenarios for making the first approach. Have the volunteers learn them verbatim and practice giving them to members of the group and then give them to someone outside the group—a friendly prospect. Make sure they follow the script and that the prospect follows the script, too—

Capital Fund Drive

TIME LINE FOR CAPITAL FUND DRIVE

July 1-31

Campaign committee is in place

   Install a powerful person as chair

   Set up divisions

   Set up head for each division (five divisions)

   Each division head has five team leaders

   Each team has five members

July 31

All organizational work is done

August

Develop campaign materials

   Brochure

   Giving clubs

   Pledge cards

   Publicity: Radio, Newspapers

   Plan events

September

Create Prospect list

   Rate prospect list

   Assign prospects to categories of giving

   Assign prospects to solicitors

October

Kickoff breakfast

October-December

   Solicitors contact prospects and ask for gifts

January

Victory dinner. Celebrate!

include rehearsing objections. This gives the solicitors a security blanket. Everyone will be able to go out and recite the script, but the highest achievers will probably use a combination of all the scripts. Their approach will become natural."

PRACTICING FOR CONFIDENCE

You can create a positive experience for your solicitors. When you have volunteers who are willing but a little hesitant, you plan a contrived experience that will always allow them to win.

You start with training sessions followed by practice—lots of practice. Your volunteers will become so drilled in the experience that their responses will become automatic. If a fundraising encounter can become like a piano recital—so well practiced that the audience can't tell you are nervous—it will be a lot easier. You don't want the presentation to sound canned. Strive for a naturalness that exudes confidence. Confidence is a key to asking for money. Training and drilling your volunteers can make them more effective.

WIN OR BREAK EVEN

Teach your volunteers that they can only win or break even. I play a little game in my workshops. It is like "Odd Man," but I change the rules. We each flip our quarters. If we match (both heads or both tails), we keep our own quarter. If we don't match, you get my quarter. After play continues for a little while, I ask, "How long would you like to play this game?" The answer is usually, "Until you run out of quarters."

The only way the other person (the one doing the asking) can lose is by not playing at all. Whenever we ask people for a gift to the library, we are starting even. When the prospect says yes, we win. If the answer is no, we haven't lost a thing. Fundraising is a "break even or win game." We can never lose.

EMPOWER TO SUCCEED

Give your volunteers the power to succeed. Use these five points to help them toward success:

1. Make expectations clear.
2. Provide necessary resources.
3. Give them authority to act independently.
4. Give them feedback while the campaign is in progress.
5. Give them the tools to measure how well they did.

REGULAR REPORTS

As the fund drive progresses, the committee meets weekly. Individual workers account to their team leader and turn in money and receipt copies on a daily basis. Team chairs stay close to their team members and report to their committee chairs, who in turn report to the chair of the drive. The secretary or treasurer makes deposits daily and keeps a running balance for reports to the group. Every donation is a success and needs to be celebrated. Use competition between teams. Have report back meetings. Praise success.

END ON TIME

End on time and celebrate. Even if you don't reach your goal by the time you said you would, end. Dragging it out won't help your cause. Invite all the workers and the big gift donors to a party to celebrate the success of your fundraiser. If you are short, perhaps one of them may kick in another $10,000 if you ask for it.

SUGGESTIONS TO HELP SOLICITORS

Here are a few ideas that may help solicitors close more deals:

Break your categories of giving into segments.
$5,000 will buy one computer terminal for the public access catalog
$2,500 will buy a printer
$1,000 will buy a laser scanner to check out books
$500 will buy three chairs
$100 will buy 10,000 bar code labels.

Offer to put their name on a piece of equipment. Immortality is a priceless commodity. You are not promising that they will live forever. You are just offering to place their name in public view for a long time. Everyone likes to be remembered.

Offer to memorialize a loved one who has died. Even if prospects don't want their own names on a piece of equipment, maybe they have loved ones they would like the public to remember.

If your are selling a book, get the person to read something from it. Cookbooks are popular fundraisers. More people buy cookbooks than ever use a recipe from them. But if they see one recipe they think they might want try, they will buy the book. If you are selling a community history book, they will look for their name. People identify with things that are familiar to them.

Try asking for a cash gift instead of selling a product. Some people would rather have a good feeling about giving to your organization than have a pound of fudge. If someone says, "I don't believe in buying raffle tickets," ask if they would like to donate $5.

Appeal to their sense of community pride. We have one of the best libraries in the whole state. Your investment can make it even better.

Appeal to their concern for children. Children are the future of our community. Please give for them.

Ask the donor for the names of other prospective donors. Sales people use this technique often. Whether your prospective donor has given or not, ask for the names of people who might be willing to give to your cause.

Ask for the prospect's help. Say: "If there were one thing I could do to help you be inclined to give to our project, what would it be?" You might get an unexpected answer, such as: "Move the book drop to a more convenient place." Or, "Plant some roses in front of the library." When you can comply with the request, do it. Then go back and ask for the gift.

DEALING WITH OBJECTIONS

How do you deal with those who say the library is already funded with tax money? They ask, "Why should I give to the library? I pay taxes. That should be enough." Chances are your prospect either is not capable of making a donation or is not that interested in the library. Start by agreeing with him. He does pay taxes, and taxes *are* the best form of support for libraries. Ask him if he wants the library to be the best it can be. Point out that taxes aren't enough to provide the level of service the community is demanding. Even though everyone pays taxes, they should also contribute a gift to the library to help it achieve a level of excellence.

PREMIUMS

Premiums are a good way to increase the number and size of the gift. If you offer a prospective donor a coffee mug for a $50 donation or a tote bag for a $100 donation, you are not selling the mug for $50 or the bag for a $100. You are offering the donor something for the contribution. It's an incentive to give, if you will. Public television, radio stations, and alumni associations seem to do the best with premiums.

If you are going to offer a premium, call it that. Don't try to *sell* a coffee mug for $50. Make sure your premiums are elegant and unusual and of the highest quality. Who wants a cheap trinket to remind them that they gave $100 to your library?

PUBLIC RELATIONS

The public relations of fundraising is not something you tack on after you develop your plans. It is woven into the fabric of everything you do. It is the invisible thread that draws attention to your project without drawing attention to itself. When you contract with a professional, the contract may have a public relations component.

Public relations are either good or bad. They can never be neutral. Good public relations is anything anyone does to create a good feeling about your library. Bad public relations is anything anyone does that detracts from your library. It could be the smile or frown on the face of the person at the front desk of your library. It could be the location of the book drop or the number of new books available.

Your fundraising campaign is a public relations activity itself. The way you conduct it will create good feelings about the library or hinder those feelings. Be aware that the potential exists to create good and bad feelings.

A library I know of raffled a used mink coat to raise money for the library. The idea of raffling a used item didn't set well with several members of the community and hampered their fundraising effort. A better choice might have been to sell the coat at auction.

Another library raised money by selling limited tickets to an Easter egg hunt. Some parents objected to paying for something that is normally a free event for children. Others were irate because limited ticket sales excluded some children from participating. The library didn't try it again.

Here are a few suggestions to keep your fundraising effort on a positive note:

- Send a regular newsletter to all potential donors. Use it to sell the services of your library. Use it to praise and recognize staff and volunteers for their efforts. Use it to make potential donors aware of the variety of giving opportunities.
- Be prepared to give a speech on your project. You will be doing the group you speak to a favor while asking them to help.
- Send news releases to the media to announce an upcoming event. Remember the key word is news. Reaching your goal is news.

- Thank the public for their support. Don't expect good coverage if it is just a promotional piece.
- Send news releases to the media to report on a successful event. Include photos, tell how much money was generated and how it will be used.
- Place paid advertising with the media. It creates goodwill with them. You can't always have your hand out.
- Say thank you loud and often. It makes people feel good to be appreciated.

PUBLIC RELATIONS AND PUBLICITY

Some people think that public relations and publicity are synonymous. They are as different as marketing and advertising. Publicity purposely draws attention to something that is happening. Public relations is the image or feeling created. Publicity is important to your fundraising effort, but for every good possible outcome, there is a negative one, too. Be careful.

News releases are great publicity if they are done well. Assign their writing to the most competent writer on your team. Poor writing belies the content of the message and sends a negative image to the reader. Newspaper editors can fix some things, but don't expect miracles. Worse yet, they can decline to print your news release if it is poorly written. Letters to the editor are good free publicity, provided all the letters support your efforts. It takes about ten positive letters to offset one negative one. Even the most positive letters can be taken in the wrong light.

SUMMARY

Soliciting donations is the most effective way to raise money for your library. You have to ask for the gift, and then wait for the prospect to respond. Learning the techniques of sound selling and applying them will help you raise the money you need for your project.

8 MEMORIALS AND DEFERRED GIFTS

On December 30th of every year, as regular as clock work, Milton Boyd brought a check to the Great Bend Public Library. Some years it was a few thousand dollars. Other years it was a little less. In his will he left 20 percent of his undivided estate to the library. He loved the library and took great delight in making his annual gift. Once in a while we took him to lunch, but mostly the staff was just nice to him when he came in. We made sure that he knew that we would be pleased to have the library named in his will.

Some may think it uncultured for a library to capitalize on the death of someone, but the library is in a unique position to offer an opportunity for lasting remembrance. Are you missing out on a steady flow of money into your library because you don't have a memorial giving program? What about bequests? Are you actively seeking them? Large bequests have been the catalyst of many library construction programs. If you are not actively seeking memorial gifts and bequests, you are missing out on two of the easiest fundraising opportunities open to you.

Do any of your current donors have estates worth over $500,000 or earn over $50,000 per year? They are good possibilities for large bequests. Board members, lawyers, and insurance agents may be able to give you some good referrals.

Try holding an estate planning clinic. Invite a lawyer, an accountant, a trust officer from a local bank, and a stock broker to sit on a panel to discuss wills and estate planning. You will be providing a valuable service, even if you don't receive a gift from one of the participants. Hold the program in the library. People who come to the library for an estate planning program may already have good feelings about the library. As you close the discussion, mention that the library is seeking deferred gifts. Send letters to all participants and thank them for coming to the program. Send your deferred giving brochure and remind them of the investment opportunity through deferred giving to the library.

All of this is an area for professional bankers, attorneys, and insurance agents. Don't try to tackle the legal complication of deferred giving, wills, estates, and insurance yourself. Unless you have someone on your board who can handle it, get good professional help.

When someone dies, friends and relatives send tokens of remembrance—usually flowers or gifts to the family or next of kin. The flowers wilt and the gift is soon forgotten. A memorial giving program creates the opportunity for donors to invest in the future of the library and extend the memory of the one who has died. It allows your donor to support your library and fulfill a social obligation at the same time. They send a gift to the library in honor of their friend or family member. You send an acknowledgment to the family and a thank you note to the donor. Everyone feels good.

The second fundraising activity I pursued in South Carolina was borrowed from the alumni newspaper of my alma mater. It was a passive appeal for memorial gifts printed on a 9 1/2" by 5 3/4" page. The headline read: "Some people believe this is a great way to honor a loved one. . . . It is." A sample memorial bookplate with the name of the donor and of the person being memorialized was placed to the left of these words. The bottom third of the flyer was a reply coupon.

When a gift came in, we sent a thank you note and a receipt to the donor and an acknowledgment to the family or next of kin. Whenever appropriate, we asked a member of the family to help us select a book to honor their loved one. We put a bookplate in the book and offered it to the donor or the next of kin before circulating it to the general public.

When Bastrop, Texas, (population 4,000), built a new library, they created a memorial gift wish list and raised $65,000 It reads, in part, like this:

Book shelving $40,000 (3 feet = $300)
Table, seat 45@ $500 each.
Reference desk $3,000
Book drop $1,000
Copier $4,500
Reading room chairs 37 @ $180 each.

They were very successful in furnishing their new library.

Memorial giving is not limited to remembering someone who has passed away. It is also a very appropriate way to honor a person for an achievement or a milestone, such as winning a contest, having a birthday or anniversary, etc. When you receive a gift honoring someone who is still living, invite him or her to help you select the book in their honor and then offer to let them be the first to borrow it. Of course, a thank you note is sent to the donor, but the acknowledgment is sent to the person being honored with congratulations on their achievement.

We put these flyers at the front desk for people to take . We also gave a few to funeral homes to give to families, hoping they would list the library as a memorial recipient in the obituary.

Great Bend Public Library
Great Bend, Kansas 67530

Presented by
Irene Pommerenky

In Memory of
Eunice Farmer

Some people believe this is a great way to honor a loved one.

It is.

The Great Bend Public Library Memorial Program is a practical, gracious, great way to pay a lasting tribute to a loved one.

You simply request that a book be added to the Great Bend Public Library in memory of a person you designate ($20 = 1 book). The library completes a memorial bookplate and secures it to the inside front cover of the book purchased with your contribution.

Result: A living memorial that will endure for years.

Complete the coupon below and mail with your check to: Great Bend Public Library, 1409 Williams, Great Bend, Kansas 67530

Enclosed is $_____ as a gift to the Great Bend Public Library. The name of the person I wish to memorialize is _____.

Please send acknowledgment to _____,

whose address is _____.

Donor's Name: _____

Donor's Address: _____

City: _____ State: _____ Zip: _____

Please make checks payable to Great Bend Public Library.

All contributions tax-deductible.

ESTABLISHING A PROGRAM.

Most libraries have de facto memorial programs, but they could do much more to increase memorial giving. Here are a few suggestions.

Start by creating a brochure. Take it to the funeral homes and ask the funeral directors to offer it to families as a possible inclusion in the obituary as an alternative to flowers or gifts. Place copies at the circulation desk of the library.

You might also try leaving copies in:

- Hospitals
- Drug stores
- Nursing homes
- Bank lobbies
- Hospices, etc.

Ask the Friends to publish it as part of their newsletter. Make a list of everyone who has ever given money to your library and send them a copy once a year.

SPREADING THE WORD

You can also advertise on the obituary page of your local newspaper. See samples at left. This will get your message before the public and remind them often. Most newspapers will give you a discount if you run the same advertisement every other day for a month. Their best rate is for an ad that runs every day for a year. You can change the ad every month to create new interest.

Once a month, publish a list of donors to the library, along with the amount of their donations, in the newspaper. Unless they request otherwise, donors like to see their names in print. Recognize them as often as possible.

Because libraries always need money for books, a memorial program that focuses on books works well. You could also establish a memorial giving registry. You would write the name of the donor and the name of the person memorialized in a special book kept on display in a prominent place in the library. Some libraries have giving clubs starting at $100 going up to $5,000 or more. Whenever someone makes a donation, the library has their name inscribed on one of the brass plates attached to the plaque. A word of caution: Make sure that all names are spelled correctly!

When you receive a gift, respond to it promptly. Send a thank you note to the donor. If you have established a book purchase

---

> **Invest in a lasting tribute with a gift to the library.**
> Great Bend Public Library

> **A memorial gift to the library is a great way to remember a loved one.**

> **A thoughtful remembrance is a memorial gift to the library.**

Send your brochure with a letter to everyone on your mailing list. Your letter could be similar to the one here. This letter is printed in 14 point type, which makes it more eye-catching and easier to read.

April 23, 1990

Dear Mr. and Mrs. Robert Cuthbert,

Here is a wonderful way to honor a loved one and invest in the future of the library at the same time. Your memorial gift in the amount of $20 or more will buy a book for the library with a bookplate honoring someone you care about.

You will enjoy the privacy of giving without revealing the amount to others. You will have the satisfaction of knowing that your gift serves a dual function. You will be helping the library and at the same time you will be remembering a friend or loved one in a fitting way. Your memorial gift to the library is a convenient way to satisfy a social obligation and tell others you truly care. Your gift is also tax-deductible.

We also invite you to honor a friend or loved one's special occasion or achievement with a gift to the library. You could say congratulations for winning a prize, or having an anniversary or birthday with a memorial gift to the library. We would be happy to honor them even further by letting them help select the book purchased in their honor.

Please keep our brochure for future use. The next time you want to remember a loved one in a lasting way, think of the library by filling out the donation form and sending it with a check of $20 or more.

Sincerely,

Librarian

memorial program, ask the donor if he or she has a subject preference. Send an acknowledgement to the next of kin as noted by the donor and offer to notify him or her when the book is ready for public circulation.

Memorial giving is tailor-made for libraries. It provides immediate cash, not just pledges of future giving. Depending on how you set it up, you can spend the money on books or anything else you want. And memorial giving is not subject to seasonal fluctuations. Deaths, birthdays and anniversaries occur all year long. Memorial giving will grow as people become more aware of your program. Once you motivate a donor to use your memorial program, he or she will tend to use it over and over. Small gifts can lead to larger gifts, even major bequests, as you develop your relationship with donors. Set up a list of all your donors and stay in touch with them with regular information about the library. This could lead to a very high return on your investment.

Use your memorial program to cultivate the next of kin as donors. After a few weeks you can send them a brief letter offering to acquaint them with the library's memorial giving program. You could say something like this. "Recently, a generous memorial contribution was made to the library in the name of ———, and we thought you might be interested in knowing more about the library and our memorial giving program. Let us know if we can help you." And so on. This type of communication can lead to larger gifts, and even a bequest in their will.

Deferred giving

As we've mentioned before, deferred giving is an attractive way for many people to donate money to their library. Often the key to obtaining this kind of gift for your library is simply asking to be included in their will.

Several years ago, the actor James Stewart gave his collection of movie scripts and manuscripts to the Brigham Young University library. When asked why he gave his collection to BYU, he responded, "Because they *asked* me, and it seemed like a good thing to do." Sometimes getting a bequest or some other form of deferred giving requires nothing more than asking. The "ask" has to come from the right person after a relationship has developed.

Donors like deferred giving because it lets them keep their money in case they need it. Deferred giving offers those whose assets are tied up in their home and other belongings an opportunity to leave a larger gift to their favorite charity—which you hope is your library.

Libraries benefit from deferred giving because it helps them develop a stable future based on larger gifts that will produce income for years to come. Deferred gifts are easier to get and tend to be larger than ordinary gifts. Libraries can use the powerful public relations of a deferred gift. A large one, well-publicized, will produce other large gifts.

TYPES OF DEFERRED GIVING

Deferred gifts are usually:

bequests in wills

life insurance or

trusts.

Lets take a look at each of these to see how a library can benefit from them.

BEQUESTS

Sometimes a librarian doesn't know that the library is included in someone's will until they die. While the librarian is appropriately grateful, think of the even greater potential had someone from the library cultivated the prospect and worked with him or her. Every library ought to be actively engaged in cultivating and soliciting deferred gifts.

You could start with a little check off box on your memorial coupon that offers more information about the library's deferred giving program. While being written into someone's will usually requires a nurturing relationship that has been cultivated over a period of several years, it starts with general awareness. Your board members could be very helpful to the library if they knew how to approach a potential donor. The best thing you can do is to make them aware of the program and give them information to share with friends. Take time to train your board members, and when an opportunity arises, they will be ready to suggest the library as a logical beneficiary to their estate.

Bequests can be cash, stocks, bonds, or real estate. In fact, I know of several libraries that own wheat farms as the result of a bequest. Another library owns an oil well. As a door opener you could try a letter of intent. It is simply a letter in which your donor says that she is going to leave the library a certain percentage of her estate or a certain dollar amount. This gives the person time to think about it, and it doesn't bind her to a commitment that she may want to change later. Once a person writes a letter of intent, she usually follows through on the commitment.

Develop a brochure that explains your deferred-giving program and distribute it widely. It is a logical extension of your memorial-giving program. Send copies of the brochure with a letter to local attorneys. They may be willing to suggest the library as a possible beneficiary to their clients. Most people want to be remembered after they die. You need to be sensitive to their feelings, but bold enough to suggest the library as a possible investment that will last beyond their lifetime.

When we organized the Great Bend Public Library Foundation in 1985, we created a brochure to help encourage deferred giving. Here's what the inside looked like. We also sent a separate giving coupon. We held an open house to announce the creation of the Great Bend Public Library Foundation. Those who came received a copy of the brochure. We also mailed out about 500 copies to people on our mailing list. One-on-one contacts are still the best.

INSURANCE POLICIES

An individual usually buys life insurance to protect the security of his or her family. Once the family is reared, life insurance is almost

PURPOSE OF THE FOUNDATION

The purpose of the **Great Bend Public Library Foundation** shall be to promote the continued growth and development of library resources and materials, and to improve the public relations and general welfare of the Great Bend Public Library. **Put simply this means more books for the Library.**

HOW WILL IT WORK?

Too often, the difficult economic times confronting the Library make necessary the curtailment of spending for its life blood, **BOOKS.** The FOUNDATION has created a fund designed to address this problem. Only the interest earned on this fund will be used for library purchases. The earnings from invested contributions to the FOUNDATION will insure a steady source of **money for books** for years to come.

A separate fund has been created to allow the donor to specify that the contribution be used by the Library for immediate purchases.

WHY GIVE TO THE LIBRARY FOUNDATION?

Because the heritage of community giving is the strength of the library.

In 1970, when we built the new library, community dollars poured in to help furnish the new building. Thousands of dollars were donated.

Every year individuals and groups give to the library for equipment and books.

Your gift to the **Great Bend Public Library Foundation** will allow the Library to continue its service to future generations.

WHAT CAN YOU DO?

Library staff and FOUNDATION board members are available to discuss with you and your advisors how you may best participate:

I. **Bequests in wills**—This is an important way to continue your concern for the Library...to share your vision with others long into the future.

II. **Gifts of Cash**

Stocks or other Securities—A present gift of stock that has appreciated in value qualifies for an income tax deduction at its fair market value. No income tax is ever imposed on the capital gain.

Real Estate

Personal Property

Life Insurance—A donor may name the FOUNDATION as the beneficiary of an insurance policy. In order to receive a current income tax deduction, one may give the FOUNDATION the policy and all ownership rights to the policy as well.

III. **Further Estate Planning Through...**

A Living Trust—Under the terms of a trust agreement a person may establish a living trust, the income from which is to provide for their needs, with all or part of the principal ultimately going to the FOUNDATION.

A Charitable Remainder Annuity Trust or Other Trust Agreements—There are a variety of flexible trusts that can serve the present needs of you and your family as well as provide a final gift for the future needs of the library.

Your tax advisor should be consulted with reference to any planned gift.

A FINAL WORD:

The citizens of this community are its most precious resource. Through **Great Bend Public Library Foundation** you can invest in their future.

As the community gives to the library, the Library gives back pleasure, enlightenment, knowledge and service to the community.

All the contributions to the FOUNDATION are tax-deductible.

worthless to a widowed spouse. If he or she possesses a paid up life insurance policy, it would be easy, and cost the person nothing, to make the library the beneficiary of the policy.

Here is another example of an insurance gift to the library. A family of modest income wanted to memorialize a child who had died. They continued a life insurance policy which was originally taken to provide cash for the child's college education. The family gave the paid-up policy to the library for an endowment to fund the summer reading program.

Someone may want to buy a policy to give the library as a means of making a large donation. Check with an insurance agent if you have someone interested in this method of giving.

TRUSTS

There are significant tax advantages to setting up a trust. One type of trust allows the donor to make a large gift to the library and receive a sizable tax deduction. The gift is invested by the library. The donor receives the income from the trust until he or she dies, and after which the charitable remainder goes to the library to use as it sees fit. Important: you will need an attorney to help set up a trust.

SUMMARY

Once you have piqued someone's interest, don't put off contacting them. You may lose the opportunity forever. If possible, use a board member or some other third party to make the initial contact after you send the letter. Your role throughout should be a supportive one. Try to be perceived as a helping counselor more than as a fundraiser. Be knowledgeable, perceptive, and low-key. If a prospective donor gets the idea that you are after his or her money, they may balk at the whole idea of giving money. Your job is to point out that a deferred gift to the library is a long-range investment opportunity.

The key to memorials and deferred giving is public awareness. If people know about your program, you will receive some money. The more widely known your program is, the more money you will receive. But like most gifts, you still have to ask for it. Board members can often be the link to those who are most likely to have large estates. Don't try to tackle a complicated legal system yourself. Get the help of a professional when it comes to trusts, wills, and deferred giving.

9 DIRECT MAIL

Would you give $50 for a fresh loaf of homemade bread? Thirty people in Great Bend, Kansas, did just that. They did it to help their library. In January 1988 the library board was facing a money crunch. We sat around the table trying to decide how to remedy a decline in city revenue. Assessed valuations were down, and the city council had done all it could to prop up our sagging budget, but we were still $10,000 short.

What could we do?

Someone thought of a fundraising letter, but our last direct-mail effort didn't generate enough donations to cover expenses. Nevertheless, we decided to try again.

We revised a letter explaining the library's plight until it fit on one page. We made up a donor card and a return envelope to send with the letter. Then we developed a list of 262 qualified, potential donors. The board discussed premiums, but everything we could afford seemed "tacky."

Believing that everyone, including the librarian, should give to their own fundraising effort, I volunteered the fruits of my avocation—fresh homemade bread. Everyone in town knows about my bread concession at the farmers' market during the summer. So I offered to deliver a fresh loaf to everyone who gave $50 or more to the library.

We mailed the letters, and money rolled in. Thirty happy donors enjoyed a loaf of fresh bread and the library was $3,100 richer. Our 262 letters won us 80 donations.

Direct mail is writing a letter to people to ask them for money. Your letter usually includes a brief statement of why you need the money and how you will use it. You usually send a donor card, a return envelope and a one page case statement only if you have an attractive drawing of the planned new building and you want to point out some benefits not included in your letter. People won't read a brochure about the library. You send this letter to people who, you hope, will give money to your library. It sounds easy. Right?

Wrong.

Andy Rooney said, "Unclear writing is a result of unclear thinking." You have to be able to state clearly and succinctly what you want to do and why people should give you money to do it. Direct mail done right takes just as much planning and effort as any other fundraising technique. The main problem with direct mail is the lack of a friendly face to ask for the gift and hold the prospect's attention while making the pitch. In fact, you have about five seconds to grab and hold the prospective donor's attention in direct-mail solicitation.

Here is a copy of the letter we sent.

Mr. and Mrs. Arthur Hillock
2341 31st Street
Great Bend, Kansas 65730

Dear Mr. and Mrs. Hillock:

Property valuations in Great Bend are down, and the library faces a substantial budget cut. Over the years, you and our other friends have used the library and enjoyed it. Now we need your help.

The library's income is based on a four-mill levy. Recent decreases in property valuations will reduce our 1988 revenue. In 1981 the people of Great Bend voted for a one-mill tax increase for the library. On April 5, 1988 the people will vote again for a mill levy increase.

Why?

Since 1983 our revenue has been more or less steady—going up one year and down the next. This situation has completely eliminated our reserve funds. Even if the vote is favorable, it will be 1989 before we receive additional tax revenue. In 1988 we need people like you to come to our rescue. We have already reduced our travel and capital outlay expenditures and cancelled a few magazine subscriptions. The book budget is next. Your gift will help us save the book budget.

We have already raised $3,000 in our fund drive. We need $7,000 more.

It will take 167 gifts of $60 each to reach our goal of $10,000. We really need several gifts of $500 or more to make this fund drive work, but your gift in any amount will be appreciated Each member of the Board has made a commitment. You can join with us in helping to keep the library a place where people get what they want.

Please send a check or make a pledge today.

Sincerely,

Delbert Sloan, President
Library Board of Directors

P.S. Our Library Director, Jim Swan, is also known for his delicious homemade bread. He is offering a premium of a fresh-baked bread, delivered to your home for a gift to the library of $50 or more.

STUDY THE PROS

How many direct-mail solicitations do you receive in a week? What do you do with them? Why not save them and study them. You can learn from the professionals by studying the direct mail solicitations you receive.

Direct mail is big business, and people make money from it. Your request has to be a little different and a little better for you to get money the same way the professionals do. Your one advantage over mass market direct mail is that people in your town know your library. I usually open mass market solicitations because once I almost threw out a replacement gas credit card because it looked like a direct mail request. Beyond that, three seconds is the maximum I spend with a direct-mail piece—unless it catches my eye. If it relates to something I am interested in, then I will spend more time with it.

Your job as a direct-mail solicitor is to get the receiver of your piece to spend more than a few seconds with your request. It will tax your skills as a letter writer and publicity design artist. You may even want to get some help. *Maximum Gifts by Return Mail* by Roland Kuniholm is worth buying and reading before you try a direct-mail solicitation.

CAUTIONARY NOTES

Before we get too deep into the business of direct mail, here are a few cautionary notes:

> Don't use direct mail in a very small town. You will be much better off organizing a few friends and informally visiting every family to ask them for money. Face-to-face contacts are much more effective. If you have a very good mailing list of people who have moved away and are still loyal to the town, you might consider a direct mail letter to them. Shirley Higgins, the board president in McCracken, Kansas, raised about $3,500 sending letters to people who had attended high school there, but had since moved away.

> Don't expect to raise a lot of money with your first letter. You will do well to break even. The first time we tried it in Great Bend we spent $425 and took in $385. Professional fundraisers say it will cost you about $1.05 to raise $1.00. So why try it at all? Because you are prospecting for new donors. You can improve the ratio of your first letter if you combine direct mail with other techniques such as follow-up telephone contacts or personal visits.

REASONS FOR WRITING

There are only about four reasons for preferring a direct-mail solicitation over contacting people face to face:

1. If you have a small donor base and you want to enlarge it.
2. If your potential donor list is large and you lack the organization and volunteers to make the face to face contacts.
3. If you have a far-reaching "alumni" list and you strongly believe they will contribute.
4. If you have already built up your direct mail donor list and direct mail is part of your annual campaign.

Direct mail is a donor prospecting tool. It will help you get the first gift. The best people to ask are those who have given to your library before. You need to move a lot of people from the list of non-givers to givers. The next step is to get them to give more.

If you are creative in developing new reasons to request money you can send out a letter up to eight times per year and make money each time.

Direct mail is a great way to contact a lot of people without involving an army of volunteers. It is work that can be done almost exclusively by paid staff—providing you have enough staff. Direct mail will also help you discover people who might give more to your cause. If someone sends you more than $50 in the mail, chances are they will give you much more when you visit them in their home or business.

CREATING THE MAILER

Since direct-mail solicitation does not have the benefits of the "human touch," whatever you send has to carry as much personality as you can put into it. It has to look as professional as possible without looking glitzy.

You start with the envelope. Any envelope from the library will probably be opened. It is best to use a windowed envelope, which always looks official. Libraries are comforting to people, so your first hurdle may not be as high as it is for other causes.

The next piece is the letter, which is the most important part. The letter is your appeal. It has to be enthusiastic, yet warm. You have to grab the reader with the first sentence and quickly draw him or her into the message. How it looks at first glance is just as important as anything you say. It has to look good.

My research revealed that people who live in small towns tend to be older than the general population. So, you should use larger print if you expect older people to read your message. For readability, it is best to use 12 or 14 point serif type. If you have to condense your message to use a larger type, so much the better.

Since the letter is the main part of your appeal, let's analyze it in greater detail.

The salutation. If you can personalize it, do it. Computers are great for personalizing mass mailings. Most word processing programs have a mail merge option that allows you to link several variables such as name, address, city, state, and zip with a letter you have written. You can even change words in the body of the letter to further personalize it.

Be careful with dot-matrix printers. Some people hate them. Letter quality is the only way to go. If all you have is a dot-matrix printer, reproduce your letter another way.

If you don't have a computer, you can still write a good letter and have it printed on your letterhead. You just won't be able to personalize the salutation. If you are thinking about putting each letter in a typewriter and typing the personal name at the top of each printed letter, forget it. That is the first place the reader's eye will focus on. It won't look good, and a generic salutation will serve just as well. Just say, "Dear friend" or "Dear Reader" or "Join us" Whatever it is, make it warm and inviting.

The lead. Your first sentence has to stand out like a friendly smile in a hostile crowd. You have to say something that interests your reader immediately. Since the library is the focal point of your request, try to associate why the person uses the library with the library's need.

Slogans work well. How about this one? "You get what you want at the library." Here are a few grabbers you might be able to use or put a twist to:

• There is no substitute for information when you want it.
• You are #1 at the library.
• They don't call us ——— for nothing.
• Only your library gives you . . .
• Your library is the best-kept secret in town.

- A little ———— can go a long way.
- Check us out.
- Information is our business.
- Children are our business.
- Say "Yes!" to your library.
- Now more than ever, you need the library. And the library needs you.
- Everything you always wanted to know about ———— is at your library.
- Turn your life around.

The body. The body has three parts—a statement of why you need the money, the appeal based on benefits to the reader or the community, and the request for the gift. Don't be subtle; ask for the gift several times.

Once you have their attention, you have to keep it with your message. By now your reader is asking, "What is the purpose of this letter?" People who already know and love the library will respond kindly to a straightforward summary of the library's need. That is how we start the Great Bend letter. You could focus on the benefits of the library to the community, but, depending on your audience, that may not be necessary. Express a sense of urgency.

Every business letter you write should focus on a single topic. In this case, the library needs money from the donor who is reading the letter. Discussing multiple issues will only confuse your reader. In the Great Bend letter, our point was: "Assessed valuations are down and the library will be forced to operate with only $10,000 in the budget if you don't help out."

Once you have outlined the need, make the appeal. Try an appeal dear to the heart of you donor. McCracken had lost its high school, so the library appealed to the alumni by offering the library as a home for school trophies and class pictures. Other appeals include:

- love of the library
- concern for reading
- love of children
- joy of life-long learning
- help for the handicapped.

Explain the benefits. The reader doesn't always have to be the direct beneficiary of the gift. Most people don't give to get a tax write-off equal to the gift—although a tax benefit is an important part of the appeal. They usually give because of some benefit to the community or a specific group they feel strongly about. Whatever the benefit, the reader needs to know who will benefit and how the money will be spent.

Ask for the money. "Please give" is a simple yet effective way to ask. "You can make the difference" is another. Or, "Every penny counts." The point of the letter is to get the reader to give money to the library for a specific project. If you don't ask for the gift in a straightforward way, they may miss the point.

Style. Involve your reader as often as possible. Ask questions. Use "You" a lot. Write from the reader's point of view. Try to align yourself with your reader by making assumptions for the reader: "We both care about the library." "I am sure you would like to see a big new beautiful library."

Create vivid word pictures. Use graphic words. What do you see when you hear, "Our library is a ghetto for books"? Or "Using our library is like crowding two people into a phone booth"? Words such as effervescent, radiant, dazzling, and glittering appeal to the senses.

Be yourself. Relax. Don't be stuffy. Put yourself into the picture—especially if you know most of the people receiving the letter. Become involved. Good writers are always visible just behind their words. If you don't care enough to become involved, your reader won't care either.

Be direct. Most people try to impress others with a profusion of words. I am impressed with brevity. Eliminate the clutter from your writing. Don't be wishy-washy. Get rid of all hedge words. If the first draft is three pages long, reduce it to a page and a half. It will be a stronger piece. Then reduce it to a page. Your fundraising letter will be more effective if you keep it short.

The close. Repeat your strongest plea for money before you sign off. You want your donor to take out his checkbook the minute he finishes reading your letter and write a check to the library.
   You might try one of these:

• You owe it to your family to give to the library's building fund.
• You will be glad you did.
• Try to imagine our library without your help.

- Think of what you have to look forward to!
- We need you . . . you need us!
- Haven't you waited long enough?
- Do it today!

Closing salutation. The person who receives the letter needs to feel a kinship with the person who wrote it. A volunteer who has nothing gain from fundraising is the best person to sign the letter—even if the librarian writes it for her. Fundraising efforts by the librarian or paid staff are often regarded as self-serving. Any tasteful closing salutation that feels comfortable will do.

The ending postscript. It may not be good style or form, but a postscript at the end of the letter gets results. It is the last impression you leave with the person who has just spent time reading your letter and considering whether or not to give you money. When a person opens a letter, the first thing they look for is their name or greeting at the top. Then they will glance quickly to the end of the letter to see who it is from. That is when they see your "P.S." While it may appear to be your last chance to convince them to give money, it may actually be your first chance. A "P.S." may be more important than the lead in your opening.

I am confident of the impact of Great Bend's postscript. After reading the "P.S." the reader probably returned to the top of the page and read the entire letter to see why the library needed him to give $50 or more. The bread offer got their attention. A 19 percent response to a direct mail piece is rare indeed. The bread turned many $25 gifts into $50 gifts.

Overall, the fundraising letter has to be short, sweet, and direct, filled with zippy words that carry the fact of the appeal as well as its emotion. It has to grab the reader from the beginning and keep her until the end. It has to make her want to write a check and send it today.

The Donation Form. Every direct mail fundraising letter must have a donor form. It can be the bottom of the page of your letter, or you can use a separate sheet. You can put your donation form on the other side of a window envelope. If someone forgets to fill out your form, you will still have their address.

The donation form must have the categories of suggested giving. Don't suggest less than $25. On a one percent return that's about what it costs you for one return gift. In the Great Bend letter we had five categories. Here is what our donation card looked like:

```
┌─────────────────────────────────────────────────────────┐
│                    DONATION CARD                          │
│   Categories of giving:                                   │
│                   Bibliofile        $500 or more          │
│                   Avid Reader         250                 │
│                   Book Worm           100                 │
│                   Steady Supporter     50                 │
│                   Magazine Peruser     25                 │
│   Enclosed is my gift of $_____                │
│                                                           │
│   Name _____        │
│                                                           │
│   Address _____        │
│                                                           │
│           _____        │
│                                                           │
│ □ Send information about making a bequest or deferred gift to the library. │
│    Your gift qualifies as a tax deductible contribution.  Thank you. │
│    Make your check payable to the **Great Bend Public Library**. │
└─────────────────────────────────────────────────────────┘
```

We received two $500 gifts, several $100 gifts, and at least 30 gifts of $50 or more, including the $500 and $100 gifts.

If you say "Give what you can," you run the risk of getting many $5 and $10 gifts and no $500 or $1,000 gifts. If someone sends you $500 in the mail, chances are they will give you a lot more if you go see them. Some skeptics say that if you suggest an amount, you will eliminate a lot of gifts or limit the top amount of giving. It doesn't work that way. You have to be sure that everyone who gets a letter understands that every dollar counts and will make a difference. Those who can't give in your lowest category will give what they can and feel good about it. Thank them just as graciously as you thank those who gave more.

The Return Envelope. Some professional fundraisers recommend enclosing a return envelope that includes permit postage. This added convenience for the donor is proven to produce more gifts. But I don't recommend it for small public libraries. The investment may not be worth the cost.

When it comes to direct-mail soliciting, there are two arguments. One is: make it as easy for the reader as you can. Those who subscribe to this idea would design the package so that all the donor had to do is to check whether he wants a green tote bag or a blue one, put his check in the self-labeled, postage-paid envelope, and mail it. The other school of thought is to require an additional commitment from the donor. Have him fill it out the donation slip and put it in his own envelope which he must address, and attach his own stamp. If he is going write a check for $25 or more, let him make the effort to get it in the mail.

I recommend stopping after the self-addressed envelope. After all, you do want the check to come to the library. And the best way to guarantee that the correct address is on the envelope is to put it there yourself.

Premiums. Premiums are an effective way to increase the number and size of gifts. You offer to give the donor something in exchange for a gift. The premium is worth only a fraction of the value of the gift. The best premiums usually serve as a reminder to the donor that she gave to an organization she cares about. And that makes her feel good. Coffee mugs, tote bags, caps, and blankets with the organizations logo on them are common examples of premiums. My alma mater offers a $100 blanket with the school's emblem on it for a gift of $500 to the athletic fund.

An $8 canvas book bag decorated with a library message might be a worthwhile premium for a $50 gift. If you know a local artist who is willing to create a special drawing of the library, you might offer reproductions of it or note cards featuring it as premiums. Plan to spend at least 20 percent of your anticipated gifts on premiums and structure your categories of giving accordingly.

Too often the premiums you can afford will be tacky and detract from your appeal. Don't use them unless you have something tied especially to your library or if you have something as unique as my homemade bread.

If you are going to use premiums and you can show a picture of what you offer, send the picture in a brochure with the fundraising letter. It will help the donor visualize the offer. If an artist has done a drawing of the library and is prepared to give reproductions of the drawing for a gift of $500, you could make a note card from the drawing and send it as a sample of the large art print. Offer a box of the note cards for a gift of $50. Offer both the note cards and art print for a gift of $500.

The package. Everything you do with direct mail must work as a single unit. The envelope should involve the reader enough to make her want to open it. The letter should inform her in a way that will make her care for your cause enough to give money with a sense of urgency. The donation card should make it easy to give. Enclosing a self-addressed envelope makes it even easier. Putting a stamp on the envelope is all right, but I don't think it's worth it.

Once you have your direct-mail package together, take one last look at it to make sure it says what you want it to say. Does it makes people feel the way you want them to feel? Does it make them feel like giving to your library?

Try giving it to a friend. Ask her to look at it through the eyes of someone who uses your library once in a while. Try these questions:

> What words or phrases do you remember?
> How would you restate what you just saw in one sentence? In a single phrase?
> Visualize the person writing this package as a movie character. What does he or she look like?
> As you read this piece, what were your unanswered questions?

The answers to these questions may be a good clue to the response to your letter. If your friend takes out her check book and writes a check for $100, you know you have a winner. Mail it. Otherwise, use your friend's comments to fix the letter. Better that one friend find a flaw in your package than that you send it to a thousand people and let each one find the flaw.

Mailing the package. It is better to put a stamp on your mailing piece than to use a bulk permit indicia. You can buy a bulk permit and buy bulk mailing stamps and use them in place of first class stamps provided you meet postal regulations for mailing bulk rate materials. You have to buy a permit. It won't be worth it if you don't plan to do a lot of mailings. Every mailing must include at least 200 pieces. And each piece must be identical to every other piece. Check with your post office before you think of a bulk mailing. It may be easier and less expensive to use first-class stamps.

The Mailing list. Who do you send a letter to? Anyone who might give you money! Start by making a list of those people who have given anything to the library before. If they have given books, magazines, memorial gifts, art works, or furniture, put their name on the list.

This list differs from the list we create for the capital drive because it includes people who live out of town. They have strong connections with your town, but are too remote for a personal contact to be practical.

Is there anyone whose name should not be on the list? Only those who live in town and might give more than $500. They deserve a face-to-face visit. Go see them in person.

Who else should go on the list. Everyone who uses the library—well, almost. Don't put children on the list. If your list isn't very long (a few hundred names or so), don't do a direct-mail solicitation. Organize your group and go see everyone in person. You will make a lot more money, and it won't cost you as much.

After you have the list, organize it and have someone find the addresses. This is a good job for staff if they aren't already too busy. Otherwise, get a committee together with the telephone book and the city directory and look up the addresses.

A final warning about the list: bring your committee together and go over it one last time. Your research is critical. Using the eyes and ears of committee members could save embarrassment and the loss of a gift. Check the list to make sure it is socially correct. You don't want to send a letter addressed to Mr. and Mrs. Bill Williams if they were recently divorced, or one or the other has just died. It is just as bad to send a "Mr. and Mrs." letter to people who have been single for years. People care a lot about the way their name is spelled. You should care too.

If I were in a small town and the library was going to do a direct-mail solicitation, I would print up all the pieces that go in the envelope and sit down with a committee of about ten people and a box of number ten, plain, white envelopes. Each of us would take a list and hand address each envelope, using the library's street number without the name as the return address. We would stuff each envelope as we addressed it and put a first-class stamp on it. No one I know has ever thrown away a hand-addressed envelope without opening it.

I know this is labor intensive, but it is effective. And you don't need a computer. Once they open the envelope, the letter has to do its job. I would start the letter:

Dear Library Friend:

The last time you were in the library, did you notice how crowded it was? We have been noticing it for years. The time has come to do something about it, and you can be a part of it by investing in our building campaign.

Our architect has designed a beautiful new 5,000-square-foot building. It will be large enough to take care of our needs for the next 20 years and beyond. With furnishings and everything, the pricetag is a cool $500,000. Right now that sounds like a lot of money, but we have already raised $300,000. We can raise the rest if everyone in town gives something.

Since this is a capital fund drive and won't be repeated, we are asking people to dig a little deeper and, if necessary, spread their gift over a three-year period. Our categories of giving start at $100. We hope you will give that much or more. Regardless of the amount of your gift, we want you to know that every dollar will be appreciated.

Your gift of $100 will buy one square foot of our new building, or it could buy five square yards of of carpeting. We have established our Honor Roll of giving. For $100 your name will be engraved on a plaque with everyone else who gave $100. We have other categories of $500 and $1,000. If you wish, you may make your donation in memory of someone dear to you.

We know you love the library and will enjoy seeing it in its new home as soon as possible. Please send your gift today. Your gift is tax-deductible.

Following the closing signature, use a postscript such as: If you send $500 or more, we will send you a 18″ x 24″ reproduction (suitable for framing) of the artist's rendering of the new library. I would put a donation card and a self-addressed envelope in with the letter and mail it.

Margaret Rawlings in Barry, Illinois, (population 1,487), needed carpeting. She said, "We wrote a personal letter to every card-holding household. Wrote newspaper articles, and talked about our needs to the community. We raised $3,000 in 19 days."

THANK YOU NOTES

When the money comes in, send thank you notes right away and record the gift in you donor file. Keep a record of everyone who has given to your library. They are your best prospects for repeat gifts. Treat them like the good friends they are.

SUMMARY

Direct mail is a great way to expand your donor base, but the first time out it will cost you more than you make. After you have a list of donors, you can send renewals and make money. The more often you send a fundraising letter to a donor, the more money you will make.

Use the following Direct Mail Planning Guide to help you do it right. Buy a book or two from the bibliography in the back of this book.

DIRECT MAIL PLANNING GUIDE

What is the overall purpose of your fundraising effort?

How does direct mail fit in with other fundraising activities?

Is your list large enough to warrant a direct-mail campaign?

Who is going to do the work? Staff? Do they have time? Volunteers? Do you have enough of them?

What method will you use to encourage prospective donors to open your letter? Premium teaser on the outside? Handwritten? Something else?

What is the main point of your letter? Why do you want the money?

What ideas do you have to grab the reader's attention? What will your lead be?

What is the emergency prompting your request?

How much money are you going to ask for?

What benefits will you offer? Name on a plaque? A premium?

Will the letter have a postscript? What will it say?

What will the package contain?

How many people do you have on your list?

Is there anyone who lives in town and might give more than $500?

What form of postage will you use? First class? Bulk rate stamps?

How will you handle the thank you notes?

Who will be in charge of recognitions?

10 GRANTS

At first, applying for a grant may seem to be an easier way to raise money for your project than soliciting funds face to face. True, you don't actually walk into someone's office and sell them on your project. You don't have to recruit a hundred volunteers to solicit donations from the community, But you are asking someone to give you money. People give to people, and your grant proposal has to be read by at least one real live person. He or she may not read more than the first paragraph. So, your skills as a salesperson now depend on your writing skills. You still have to research the prospect. Writing a grant proposal does not relieve you of the need to get to know the people who will be making a decision about your application.

You have to critically assess the needs of your organization and evaluate your project. Performance still precedes funding. If your feasibility study reveals a lack of local support for your library, don't try to shift your fundraising effort to grant writing. It will likely fail. The weaknesses reflected in your preliminary study will also come out in your grant proposal. Writing a successful grant proposal requires just as much planning as any other fundraising method.

Can you state the mission of your library clearly and succinctly? Can you describe what you want to do in 25 words or less? Do you know exactly how much it will cost? Can you tell who will benefit from your project? If you can, give yourself a green light and put your idea for a grant through the planning process.

Grant writing is currently a hot topic on the workshop circuit. You can spend two or three days and hundreds of dollars learning how to be a grant writer. If you can't get to a workshop, buy one or more of the hundreds of books available and teach yourself how to be a grant writer. Two books I highly recommend are *Getting Funded: A Complete Guide to Proposal Writing* by Mary S. Hall and *Foundation Fundamentals: A Guide for Grant Seekers*, 3rd edition by Patricia Read.

Grants for Libraries and Information Services, published by the Foundation Center, is a well-organized tool specific to libraries. It is one of 23 COMSEARCH: Broad Topics culled from the Foundation Center's database of over 43,000 grants of $5,000 or more in a wide variety of subject and geographic areas. It lists actual foundation grants, reported to the Foundation Center. By examining these foundation grants you can identify those independent, corporate, and community foundations whose giving interests match your institution's funding needs. *Grants for Libraries and Information Services* will help you to:

- develop a viable list of funding prospects
- identify other institutions or programs whose interests are similar to you own—and have been funded
- pinpoint foundation giving trends in the library field.

This resource can save you time by helping you to avoid applying to foundations whose giving interests do not fall within your subject area or geographic location. A study of this book will tell you that not very many small public libraries receive grants of $5,000 or more. It may be because they don't apply, or it could be that they have received smaller grants that are not reported in *Grants for Libraries and Information Services*.

In their book, *The Art of Winning Foundation Grants*, Howard Hillman and Karin Abarbanel give ten steps to success:

1. Define your goal.
2. Assess your chances.
3. Organize your resources.
4. Identify your prospects.
5. Research your prospects in depth.
6. Make your initial contact.
7. Meet with the foundation.
8. Write your formal proposal.
9. Submit your formal proposal.
10. Follow up.

Notice that writing the formal proposal is almost at the end of the list. Too often, enthusiastic people are prone to "action outbursts." They want to solve the problem immediately, without taking the time to assess the situation and plan appropriate action.

Books and workshops can teach you the right things to say and how to apply where you are most apt to be funded. The consulting staff of your state library or system may be able to help you with a grant application, too. Don't try to do it all on your own. Buy or borrow the books. Attend a workshop. *Get some help*—especially if this is your first grant proposal.

THE FOUNDATION CENTER

One of the best places to get help is the Foundation Center. The Foundation Center is an independent national service organization established by foundations to provide an authoritative source of information on private philanthropic giving. The Center disseminates information on private giving through public service programs, publications and through a national network of library reference collections for public use. The New York City, Washington, D.C., Cleveland, and San Francisco reference collections operated by the Foundation Center offer a wide variety of services and comprehensive collections of information on foundations and grants. Cooperating collections include libraries, community foundations and other nonprofit agencies that provide a core collection of Foundation Center publications and a variety of supplementary materials and services in areas useful to grant seekers.

Over 100 of the network members have sets of private foundation information returns (IRS Form 990-PF) for their states or regions that are available for public use. A complete set of returns from all 50 states can be found at the New York City and Washington, D.C. offices of the Foundation Center. The Cleveland and San Francisco offices contain IRS returns for those foundations in the Midwestern and Western states, respectively.

Call each collection before you visit them. Collections operated by the Foundation Center are:

The Foundation Center
312 Sutter Street, Room 312
San Francisco, CA 94108
415-397-0902

The Foundation Center
1001 Connecticut Avenue, NW
Washington, DC 20036
202-331-1400

The Foundation Center
79 Fifth Avenue
New York, NY 10003
212-620-4230

The Foundation Center
Kent H. Smith Library
1442 Hanna Building
Cleveland, OH 44115
216-861-1933

A call to any one of these centers can put you in touch with the nearest cooperating collection.

Anne Borland of the Foundation Center in New York City gives three tips for getting a foundation grant:

1. Obtain a list of libraries that participate in the Foundation Center's cooperating collection.
2. Secure a computer search of foundations that have funded grants for libraries and information projects.
3. Check with the librarians in the libraries with cooperating collections. They usually have a broad range of helpful suggestions and ideas.

Most state libraries and regional library systems have professional consultants who can help you on a variety of library funding matters. They can help with writing your grant application.

CUSTOMIZING YOUR PROPOSAL

Before you get all excited about writing a grant proposal, remember that many other people will also be applying. Applying for a grant is like looking for a job. The funding agency is the employer, and you are the applicant. In a hiring situation, the employer is looking for the applicant who best matches the job requirements. Your task is to learn as much as you can about the company and the job and create the image that your qualifications match the job requirements. The most effective resumes are rewritten to match the specific requirements of each job. You can't change your education or work experience, but you can emphasize those aspects of your career that match the employer's job announcement.

Be sure your grant applications are appropriate. Don't seek a grant to buy computers from a foundation that has only given grants for new building construction. You need the kind of help you can find in books like *The Foundation Directory* and the *Corporate Foundation Profiles,* both published by the Foundation Center. Many states have published a directory of foundations for their state. Check with the Foundation Center's Cooperating Collection in your state to see if your state has one. These directories list agencies which award grants within the state. Make sure you have the latest edition. A three-year old directory is practically worthless. Foundation directories include the following types of information:

• correct name of agency
• street address

- telephone number
- establishment data
- year-end date of accounting period
- assets of agency
- total expenditures
- amount and number of grants paid
- types of grants and other types of support
- sample of grants given (Recipient and amount)
- geographic limitations
- subject limitations
- types of support limitations
- printed materials available from agency
- application information
- person to whom proposals should be addressed
- officers
- staff
- IRS Identification Number.

Not every agency listed in every directory gives all of the above information, but the information they do give will help you decide where to apply.

Grant seekers need to match their applications to the giving profiles of funding agencies. As many as 75 percent of all grant proposals are rejected simply because they were in the wrong place. Either the grant writers had not done their research, or they were hoping against hope to receive funding from an agency that had never funded similar proposals before. These misdirected proposals are not funded because they weren't well-written or the need wasn't well established. They simply didn't match the grant requirements of the funding agency. When matching your need with the the grant requirements, pay meticulous attention to the following:

Geographic limitations. This is a tough one to overcome. If your library is outside the geographic requirements of the granting agency, don't waste your time. Several years ago I was helping my oldest son apply for college scholarships. We went through several books that listed aid to college students. It was frustrating to read about a great scholarship and then see in the fine print: "Grants limited to residents of Clark County"—not our home county.

Many private foundations have narrow geographic restrictions. It is great if you live within the granting area. Libraries in Cloud County, Kansas, regularly receive grants from a private foundation that funds only organizations in the county. The grants aren't large, but they help buy equipment and other big ticket items small libraries can't afford. If you live in the area specified by the agency or if you are sure no geographic restrictions apply, you have a green light to the next intersection.

Subject limitations. Some foundations refuse to fund religious organizations or campaigns to eliminate or control specific diseases. Other grant funders may support only agencies dealing with the youth or the elderly or a specific ethnic group. Grant agencies that fund educational institutions may also award grants to public libraries. It depends on the skill of the grant writer. Check to see if any public libraries have been awarded grants in the past few years. If not, you could be the first, but don't count on it.

Types of support. Some funders will provide operating budgets, seed money, and emergency aid. Others are into the business of grants for buildings only. Some will not give money for research, publications, films, conferences, or travel. Your job is to find a grant funder that will provide the type of support you need and apply there.

Amount of funding. A foundation or other grant funder that has made grants to libraries of your size for equipment in the past year is a good prospect for your automated circulation system. If their largest grant was for $5,000, you probably cannot expect to find all the money you need in one place. You need to know how much money they have given to libraries like yours and for what purpose.

Sources of regular funding. Some foundations refuse to give money to agencies that receive taxes. The rationale is that access to tax funds insures adequate funding. (You may not agree with that policy, but it is their money.) Other grants are only available to publicly supported libraries. Try these agencies. You will have a much better chance.

Other special considerations. One of the scholarship sources we explored for our son was a private foundation in New England. Recipients had to be of English or German descent. They could not attend classes that would prepare one for the ministry. Every year, if they were in the United States, recipients had to attend a special memorial service at the grave site of their benefactor. Not every grant agency has such complicated restrictions. Be careful that the restrictions don't offset the value of the grant.

Your job is to uncover the best possible funding sources and then develop a proposal that will be funded. Printed materials are helpful. You will be surprised how much you can learn from a copy of a newsletter or annual report. If the funding agency encourages a preliminary query letter, write one. Try to find out as much as you can before you start writing your grant proposal.

GETTING THE EDGE
Here are some suggestions that may help give you an edge at winning grant funding.

Call the secretary of the funding agency. Ask for guidelines for submitting a grant proposal. Ask for suggestions or ideas. Try to find out what makes a difference to the grant readers. For example: The people on the grant awards committee may hate anything typed on a dot-matrix printer, etc.

Contact your regional Foundation Center Cooperating Collection. Many are housed in libraries and have trained librarians who can direct you to many sources on grant writing and fundraising.

Obtain copies of 990-PF report. This is the form each foundation must file with the IRS each year. Copies are available from the state attorney general's office. Limited copies may be available through your regional Foundation Center.

Secure a computer search. The database of the Foundation Center publications is available through DIALOG. You can tailor your search to meet the needs of your project.

Call former recipients of grants. If they are not applying again, they may be willing to give you a few pointers.

Tom McGavran, a member of the Delphos (Kansas) Lions Club, was responsible for writing a successful grant proposal to the Lions Club International Foundation. His effort netted the local club the largest grant ever awarded in Kansas by the International Foundation. His practical advice may help other grant seekers. Here are his suggestions:

- Find out what kinds of projects the foundation has funded in the past.
- Start with a project that reflects a serious community need.
- Have firm commitments for the local share of the match.
- Provide as much detail as possible.

• Stay in touch with the secretary who accepts the grants.
• Make sure the grant application is complete before you send it in.

TYPES OF GRANTS

Grants are available from a variety of funding agencies, including the federal government. The possibilities include:

Tax supported grants:
    LSCA Title I-Library Services
    LSCA Title III-Interlibrary Cooperation and
    LSCA Title II-Public Library Construction

Resource Sharing:
    LSCA Title VI-Library Literacy
    Older Americans Act
    State competitive/incentive grants
    State grants-in-aid

Foundations:
    Private
    Civic
    Corporate
    Local
    National
    Banks

LIBRARY SERVICES AND CONSTRUCTION ACT

Most LSCA titled funds are administered by the state library agency in each state. The LSCA Advisory Council is appointed to help the state librarian administer these funds. Every state is different. Some states encourage wide open competition for a variety of LSCA grants, while other states use LSCA funds to maintain ongoing cooperative programs, such as interlibrary loan or continuing education. Competition is discouraged. Find out how your state administers LSCA funds. Then do everything you can to get your share. You may have to make a trip or two to the state capital, but it will be worth it in the end, when your project is funded.

The current year of the *Catalog of Federal Domestic Assistance* belongs in your library. It outlines everything you ever wanted to know about federal grants. All entries follow this basic outline:

federal agency
authorization
objectives
types of assistance
uses and restrictions
eligibility requirements
application and award process
assistance considerations
post assistance considerations
post assistance requirements
financial information
program accomplishments
regulations and guidelines
information contacts
related programs
examples of funded projects
criteria for selecting proposals.

Although only a few of the programs listed apply to public libraries, the information on those few programs is important to you. Other nonprofit agencies in your community will benefit from this publication, too.

LSCA TITLE II—PUBLIC LIBRARY CONSTRUCTION

This is the most visible competitive grant program for libraries. The application form is fairly lengthy, but not insurmountable. I have written several successful proposals and assisted with others. The key to success is being present at the meeting where the grants are made. Most states have open meetings laws. You have a right to be there. Make a short speech if the awards committee will let you. Cry if you think it will help. If they give you five minutes to highlight your proposal, take four. Your brevity will be appreciated. Bring visuals, preferably a vision of what you plan to build, rather than one that shows how bad your old library is.

On the other hand I have seen beautifully prepared proposals with visuals and graphics that were not funded at all because they didn't have their matching funds in the bank. If you want to build a $250,000 library, try for a $100,000 grant, but you better have a similar amount in the bank drawing interest and the rest in pledges. An approved bond issue is just as good. Those who approve your grant like to see that you have been working to raise money at home. They might be willing to put you over the top with a LSCA grant, but they won't provide the lead gift.

Be aware that Title II grants in excess of $25,000 require a special audit. That audit can cost $2,000 or more. Plan for it in your budget.

Be prepared to answer the following questions if you are going to apply for a LSCA Title II Public Library Construction Grant:

Section I
Legal name of applicant.
   Address.
   Congressional district.
   County.
   Name, title, address, and telephone number of person completing this application.
   Copy of statute under which the library was established.
   In what year was the library legally established?
   Is the board of trustees appointed according to state statute?
   Are the library's financial records audited annually by a licensed municipal or certified public account?
   What is the library's mill levy for the last completed year?
   What is the library's source of public support?
   What is the library's maximum mill levy?
   Revenue from local tax sources for the last completed year. Attach a copy of the budget.
   Per capita tax support for the last completed year.
   Other revenue for the library's operation. (Do not include gifts to help with construction project.)
   What cooperative arrangements does the library have with other libraries or regional systems.
   Is the board willing to comply with the Civil Rights Act of 1964, Public Law 88-352 (42 U.S.C. 1971 et. seq.), and all amendments thereto?
   Will free library services be offered from the new or remodeled facility?
   How well does your present facility meet standards in the following area:

   Number of hours open per week?
   Number of professional librarians employed?
   Number of college graduates employed?
   Number of library assistants employed?
   Number of clerical persons employed?

Number of shelvers employed?
Total number of persons employed?

How will the planned facility meet the standards in the following areas:

Number of hours open per week?
Number of professional librarians employed?
Number of college graduates employed?
Number of library assistants employed?
Number of clerical persons employed?
Number of shelvers employed?
Total number of persons employed?

List the name(s) of the positions and give the education and or experience of each person employed by the library. Include vacant positions.

Describe the plan or plans, if any, for additional or new personnel to be employed in the new or remodeled facility.

Section II
Geographical and population data:

Name(s) of neighborhood, city, township, county, district, and/or region served by your library.
Population served by your library.
Predominant characteristics of area served (urban or rural).

Section III
In what year was the present facility constructed?

Has the present facility been condemned or declared structurally unsafe by an engineer or architect?

If yes, give name and address of person who made this determination and attach a copy of their report.

If this project is remodeling or adding on to an existing facility, attach a statement from an architect or engineer stating the structural soundness of the existing facility.

Will proposed library facility be attached to another facility or be constructed as part of another facility?

If yes, give description.

If yes, will the proposed library have its own outside entrance?

If a new facility or an addition is planned, has the site been acquired?

If yes, give the legal description of the land.

All applicants will comply with the requirements of Title II and Title III of the Uniform Relocation Assistance and Real Property Acquisitions Act of 1970 (P.L. 91-646) which provides for fair and equitable treatment of persons displaced as a result of Federal and federally assisted programs.

The new or remodeled facility will be designed to comply with the *American Standard Specifications for Making Buildings and Facilities Accessible to, and Usable by, the Physically Handicapped.* Number A117.1-1961, as modified (41 CFR 101-17.703).

Give the amount of funds *on deposit* for the project.

Specify the source of local matching funds on deposit.

If local matching funds have been or are being obtained through the sale of bonds or a building levy, cite the statute authorizing such.

If local matching funds were obtained as the result of a bond issue, attach a copy of the proposition as presented to the voters. Attach a certified copy of the results of the election.

If the local matching funds are being collected under a special building levy, attach a certified copy of the resolution, as published, authorizing such levy. If an election was required, attach a certified copy of the results of the election.

Give the amount of additional local matching funds anticipated.

Estimate the date on which anticipated local matching funds will be available for the project.

Specify the official governing body which will administer the local matching funds available for the project.

Section IV

This project is:

> Construction of a new facility.
> Addition to an existing facility.
> Remodeling of an existing facility.
> Addition to and remodeling of an existing facility.

This facility will be used as a:

> Main or central unit.
> Branch.
> System headquarters.
> Processing center.
> Other (specify).

Name and address of project architect.
Name and address of building consultant.
Type of ownership.
Preliminary estimates of construction costs—total funds from local and federal sources budgeted by categories:

Administrative costs	$_____
Architect's fees	$_____
Site acquisition	$_____
New construction	$_____
Acquisition of existing facility	$_____
Remodeling of existing facility	$_____
Equipment and furniture	$_____
Other, (specify)	$_____
Total	$_____

Preliminary financial analysis of total funds as reported above budgeted by source:

Local matching	$_____
LSCA Title II	$_____
Total	$_____

Source and estimated amount of local matching funds, as reported in the above amount, available to the applicant for this project

Cash or appropriation	$_____
Bonds	$_____
Special building levy	$_____
Pledges and/or donations received	$_____
Contingent donations, pledges	$_____
Total	$_____

Floor space in square feet of present facility.
Floor space in square feet of new or remodeled facility.
Estimated volume and seating capacity before and after project completion.
Give projected time line for construction and completion.

In narrative form, describe the inadequacies of the present facility. Include any features of the building which prohibit use by or present hardship to the physically handicapped. Narrative should be based on *Interim Standards for Small Public Libraries or Minimum Standards for Public Library Systems, 1966.*

In narrative form, describe the proposed facility. Include information regarding the location of the site, parking facilities, esthetics of the building, etc. Narrative should be based on *Interim Standards for Small Public Libraries or Minimum Standards for Public Library Systems, 1966.* Attach a copy of your written building program and preliminary drawings or blueprints.

Equipment and furniture: List existing equipment, if any, which will be used in the proposed facility. Describe new equipment and furniture to be purchased and indicate its use in the proposed facility.

Describe in narrative form the plan of services for the proposed facility. Narrative should include present services and projected services, and a budget summary showing projected services.

Show on a map the total area your library is serving or plans to serve, including areas that are outside your present taxing district. Indicate which areas are in the present taxing district and which are outside the present taxing district.

The application also includes a very long list of federal assurances the library must agree to in order to be eligible for a grant. The form of the application may vary from state to state, but the information and assurances required are the same in each state.

All the paperwork notwithstanding, the LSCA Title II Public Library Construction program is one of your best chances to receive a grant to complete your building project. Don't pass it over just because you don't want the paperwork hassle. The extra work is worth it, even if you just want to make your rest rooms accessible to the handicapped. Check with the person in the state library who is responsible for overseeing LSCA funds. He or she will be able to give you all the details.

LIBRARY LITERACY

This is one of the few federal grants awarded directly to public libraries. The objectives of this grant are "to provide support to State public libraries for coordinating and planning library literacy programs and making arrangements for training librarians and volunteers to carry out such programs; and to provide support to local public libraries for promoting the use of voluntary services in providing literacy programs, acquiring materials for literacy programs, and using library facilities for such programs." Applications are evaluated by outside experts and library program staff. Awards are made to eligible state and local public libraries by the Secretary of Education. Competition for these grants is fierce, but very rewarding if you are funded.

You can use the grant to provide training for librarians and volunteers to teach adults to read. You can also use the money to buy materials you plan to use in connection with your literacy program.

If you are interested in a literacy grant, pay particular attention to the criteria for selection proposals. Which are:

> plan of operation
> quality of key personnel
> budget and cost effectiveness
> evaluation plan
> adequacy of resources
> cooperation and coordination.

You can't build a new library with literacy grant money, but it is a terrific way to build your image in the community and to recruit and train volunteers. Try cooperating with the your local community college. They may have a full time grant writer. Working together, you can create greater visibility for both of you.

OLDER AMERICANS
The Older Americans Act is designed to provide special library programs for the elderly. Public libraries can apply through the state library to fund programs specifically targeted for the elderly. Large-print books, low-vision aids, and programming materials for the elderly are possibilities for this grant.

STATE COMPETITIVE/INCENTIVE GRANTS
The Interlibrary Loan Development Program in Kansas is one of the few state-funded competitive grants to libraries. It is designed to foster interlibrary cooperation through grants to purchase materials that can be used for interlibrary loan.

In Illinois, per capita incentive grants are awarded based on public library performance, according to some of the criteria outlined in *Output Measures for Public Libraries*. If your state offers similar grants, you should be aware them through your state library. Try to attend the meeting where the awards are made—especially if grants are competitive rather than based on performance measured against a fixed criteria. Your presence is a powerful factor in the process. If committee members have questions about your application, you will be there to answer them.

FOUNDATIONS AND CORPORATIONS
Only about ten percent of all charitable giving comes from foundations and corporations. Libraries receive a small percentage of

that. But the pie is still very large, so don't despair. If after careful research, you think you can qualify for a foundation grant, go for it.

The application for a small local grant may be as simple as writing a letter. You simply:

- Tell who you are.
- Define your need.
- State what you want to do.
- Tell how you are going to accomplish it.
- Ask for a specific amount.

If you have received a grant from this foundation before, write the letter and ask for the money. You will need a more carefully developed proposal if you are going for a sizable grant from an untried source. If they don't have a form to complete you will have to organize your own proposal.

Here is a basic outline using as an example the need for a new building:

Identify your organization. We are a public library in a town of 50,000

Give a little history. The library was built in 1939 under a WPA program.

Identify your problem. Our 50-year-old library is overcrowded and in need of repair

Document your specific need. The library was built to serve 5,000 people. It was remodeled and expanded to 15,000 square feet in 1953. The standard for a library in a town our size is 25,000 square feet. There is no room for expansion in our present location.

State your objectives. We want to build a new 25,000-square-foot building near the population center of our town.

Describe your activities. The site has been selected and has received enthusiastic support from the community. We have a contract with a local architect to design the building. A local fundraising committee has been formed, and the bond election is scheduled for next spring.

Describe the required resources. The estimated cost of the building is $2,500,000. (Include a copy of the budget with antici- pated revenue by source.)

Outline the plan of evaluation. Our project will be successful when people can enjoy the new library.

CORPORATE GRANTS

Corporate giving is based on a desire to help employee families. If you are applying for a corporate grant, emphasize the benefits to the employees of the corporation. Does a major corporation have a production plant in your area? Has it made grants to agencies like yours before? Write to corporate headquarters and apply for a grant. If nobody in your town works for the XYZ Corporation and they don't have a plant within 50 miles of your town, don't waste your time submitting a grant proposal.

Kanopolis, Kansas, (population 653), got a new library in three phases thanks to a local salt mine. The mining company paid to have the shell of a metal building erected (phase I). The library and the community finished the inside and furnished it.

The building wasn't large enough to include a meeting room, so they added a meeting room and kitchen and expanded the rest rooms (phase II). A few years later, the children's department outgrew its space, so the salt company added a new meeting room (phase III) and the old meeting room became the children's department.

Many foundations and corporations require a copy of the letter from the IRS designating your library as a 501 (c) 3 agency. If you don't have the letter you will have to fill out forms 1023 and 872- C. You can obtain these forms from the Internal Revenue Service. (See Chapter 14.)

CIVIC FOUNDATIONS

Most international major civic groups—Lions, Rotary, Kiwanis, Optimists, etc.—have a foundation that is funded by donations of the member clubs. They make grants to local clubs for needed nonprofit projects. The Lions in Delphos, Kansas, received a matching grant from the Lions Clubs International Foundation to help remodel an old bank building into a library and a meeting room. If you can team up with one of these groups they may be able to secure a grant to help with a library project.

WRITING YOUR PROPOSAL

When you write your grant proposal remember:
  Keep it simple.

Be brief.

Don't use jargon.

Get a copy of *The Elements of Stye* by William Strunk and E.B. White. It is one of the most clearly written books on the subject of writing. *Writing with Precision* by Jefferson D. Bates takes the next step. Bates suggests using the active voice in preference to the passive voice. This means the subject performs the action rather than being acted upon. Note the difference in the following examples:

Active voice: The fundraising committee raised a million dollars.

Passive voice: A million dollars was raised by the fundraising committee.

Get to the heart of things as soon as you can. Don't skip any points, but avoid spending too much time with any one point. You have to establish basic information about your library and its need, but don't overdo it.

Put yourself in the place of the grant proposal reader. Reading a stack of 100 grants just like yours would make you tired. Would you want to read every last word of every proposal? Probably not! Do yourself and the grant reader a favor. Start by writing your grant proposal the way you normally write. Then cut it in half. You will have a better document.

Try using a semi-outline style. Separate your main points into paragraphs. This style is more open and accessible to the reader. Judge for yourself. Which of the following selections is easier to read?

This:

> We need a literacy program in our community because 30 percent of the adult population reads at or below the fourth-grade level, the first language of ten percent of the people is not English, and 40 percent of adults are not high school graduates.

Or this:

> We need a literacy program in our community because:
> - 30 percent of the adults can't read above fourth grade level.
> - 10 percent speak English as a second language.
> - 40 percent have not graduated from high school.

You are not writing masterful prose. You are writing a grant proposal and you want it to be funded. It won't be funded if it isn't read. No one will read it if they have to hunt for your main points.

Get to the bottom line quickly and repeat it again at the end. In the first paragraph or in a cover letter, tell them how much money you want and why. The rest of your proposal will support and document your request. Don't make your reader wait till the end to discover the most important part.

It also helps to have a *shtick*—a special gimmick that makes you stand out above the rest. If you want to be noticed in a crowd, you wear a red dress or sport a wild tie. I don't mean that you should submit your grant on dayglow orange paper. I do suggest developing a style of writing that is easy to read and filled with unique, graphic, even humorous word-pictures. Your grant proposal will look just like everyone else's unless you do something to make it special.

Picture a 300-pound man barely squeezing through a library door because it wouldn't open more than a few inches. One of the LSCA Title II Public Library Construction grants I helped write for a library in our system included the following statement: "Jim Swan can barely squeeze through the front door of our present library." Truth was, everyone who came to the library had to go through the doorway sideways. A large man squeezing through the door of the library created an effective word image. The grant was funded at 100 percent.

SUMMARY

Don't hang all your hopes for fundraising on a grant. You will likely be disappointed. Only one in ten grant applications is funded. At best, grants will form only a small portion of your total fundraising portfolio. The basics of research, planning, and organization still apply. Grant proposals are like resumes. You are trying to sell your idea to someone by proving that what you want to do is the same thing your funder wants to do. Your funder has the money, and you are going to do the work. If you are serious about grant writing as a fundraising activity, get help from workshops, books, and other professionals.

11 ANNUAL EVENTS

In Youngstown, New York, (population 4,721), the library raises over $9,000 each year by going door-to-door in the community. Volunteers make personal solicitations, and letters are sent to previous patrons and sponsors. The community feels part of the library, committed to its success. This annual event flourishes because people have come to expect it.

Annual events are successful because customers come back year after year. Common examples of annual events are used book sales or arts and crafts fairs.

The most important ingredient of an annual event is its regularity. Downtown merchants often have a sidewalk sale the last Thursday in July, come rain or shine. People count on it. They save their money and look forward to it. They enjoy repeating a positive, pleasurable experience.

An annual event differs from a capital fund drive in that it occurs every year. A capital fund drive is designed to raise a lot of money in a short period to build a new library or some other capital-intensive project. Annual events assume an ongoing need for money. Many college foundations run their annual giving campaigns like capital fund drives and invest the proceeds for scholarships. Libraries don't offer scholarships, but they buy books and other capital intensive equipment and may have high ongoing maintenance costs.

Any fundraising activity could become an annual event. In fact, all annual events started out as single money-making activities. They were so successful that those running them said, "Let's try that again." Soon the fundraising committees became the fashion show luncheon committee or the pancake feed committee or the book sale committee. These committees became very proficient in organizing and carrying out the annual event. After the completion of each year's carnival or luncheon, they sat down and evaluated. They asked, "What went well?" "What could we do better?" Their answers helped plan and refine next year's event.

When we persist in doing something, it becomes easier for us to do. The task itself is not changed, but our power to do it is increased. We become good at annual events because we do them over and over again. The better we become, the easier they are for us to do and the more money we make doing them.

Diana Stern, the librarian in Woodstock, New York, (population 6,823), says, "Our major fund raiser is our annual Woodstock Library Fair which is held on the last Saturday of July (rain or shine). We sell used articles of all sorts—books, clothes, furniture, you name it; we have a large raffle with a trip as the first prize; there is entertainment and food; a special "kiddieland" is created

153

for children's entertainment. Since this fair has been going on for about 60 years, you see we really have a tradition on our side. All of the work is done by volunteers. This event brings in about $25,000, but it costs about $6,000 to put on. We ask for an admission donation at the gate."

Joyce Anschutz is one of the best first grade teachers I know. She has taught the first grade for more than 15 years—perfecting her skills and methods over the years. Each fall she gets a new batch of six-year-olds. Teaching, for her, is like a year-long annual event; an experience she repeats year after year. She gets better every year because she doesn't have to learn how to teach beginning reading again. All she has to do is review and prepare for the contingencies.

If you have an annual fundraising event, it won't be long until all you have to do will be to update and plan for contingencies. Annual fundraising events are great because people like them and count on them. You will become proficient at making them successful.

SELLING VERSUS SOLICITING GIFTS

If you are going to sell something to make money for your library, the best thing to sell is something you don't have to buy. That insures a 100 percent profit. The only reason we should sell things to raise money is to get money from nonconstituents. If we expect most of our money to come from our constituents, why not just ask them for a donation? One day at church I was asked to make 100 loaves of bread to raise money for the missionary fund. I refused, not because I didn't want to support the missionary fund, but because I knew that the people who would buy my bread would also give to the missionary fund without the bread.

Churches hold all kinds of fundraisers that draw people from outside their faith to contribute to their building fund, or missionary fund, etc. You don't have to be a Mennonite to enjoy famous Mennonite cuisine or buy one of their beautiful quilts. You just have to have enough money, which they will be glad to exchange for their food or handiwork.

It seems easier for some people to sell something than to solicit gifts or ask for donations. The psychology of offering something of worth at fair value is soothing to the soul of the seller. Perhaps it harks back to our feelings of working for what we get rather than begging for it. Do we feel that asking for a gift for the library is begging? Do we feel that by offering something tangible in return for their money we have earned or worked for the money? Maybe so. Perhaps that is why some of us would rather sell something to earn money rather than ask for a gift outright.

Let's take an honest look at the ever-present bake sale. People will spend $3 or $4 for the ingredients to make a cake, spend an hour or two making the cake, and then give it to the bake sale to be sold for $5. Wouldn't it be easier to donate the $5 and not have the work of making the cake? Or worse yet, face the prospect of buying our own cake back for $5?

If you buy something with the idea of selling it for a profit, you run the risk of losing your investment. A nonprofit group in Minneapolis, Kansas, (population 2,000), has a closet full of drink squeeze bottles they would like to get rid of—at cost.

CHARGE ENOUGH TO MAKE MONEY

The biggest problem money-making projects have is not charging enough. We are trying to make money for our libraries, not offer a bargain. A fair price is whatever a willing buyer and a willing seller agree upon. If no one complains about the price, you are probably not charging enough. If someone is going to buy something from you to help your organization, and you are selling something they want, any price under $10 will not deter them. The pricing rule of thumb I use with my bread business is four times the cost of the materials. If you can't make something and sell it for at least four times the cost of the materials, don't bother. Your labor is worth more than that. Find another activity.

A while back, two young women at church asked me to buy one of the cookbooks they were selling for a fundraising project.

"How much?" I asked.

"$5.75," they replied.

I said "Okay," without asking to see one.

When I asked how much they had paid for them, they said, "About $2.90." The publisher had suggested selling them at $6.25. I suggested $6.50. Seventy-five cents on a cookbook doesn't sound like much, but if you are selling a thousand of them, that's $750. If you are selling something for a fundraiser, you will probably sell just as many at an inflated price as you will at a discounted price. Most people feel they are making a donation to the cause, not shopping for the best price possible, so why not capitalize on their generosity?

I don't recommend becoming retail agents for a wholesaler. Neither do I believe in exploiting children by making them solicitors for the library. When my oldest son was in junior high school, he became involved in a money-making scheme for the student council. Students went door-to-door selling summer sausages and specialty cheese products. The company offered inexpensive premiums as incentives to the students. When the merchandise arrived the students delivered it and collected the money. The student council made a healthy profit.

Sounds like a good deal for everyone, right? Wrong.

Guess who made the most money? The people who sold the sausage to the school.

Guess who did most of the work? The students.

They were selling a $4 sausage for $6 (I checked it out at the supermarket). They were helping the manufacturer retail his product at an inflated price.

If you are going to buy something and sell it as a money-making project, check it out carefully before you sign a contract or send money. First of all, figure out what the product is selling for in the store. Then figure out what the manufacturer is charging you for the privilege of selling his product. If you are selling something for $6 and you get to keep 40 percent, you are paying $3.60 for the product. If you can buy it in the store for $3.75, chances are the merchant bought it for $3 or less. If you can't make at least a 50 percent profit and compete with the stores on price, find something else to sell.

Try not to compete with the stores at all. It's not nice to sell something they sell and then go around asking them for a donation. Try to find something unique or make it yourself. That way you can charge whatever you want.

Do your homework before jumping into a money-making deal with a supplier. Will your community buy whatever it is you are planning to sell? This is the point of community-based fundraising: discover something the community needs, make it yourself, and sell it. Or capitalize on a local resource or talent and export your product. Not all of the money for your library has to come from the community.

The question then becomes what to sell. If you make something unique and sell it, everyone wins. A woman in Great Bend has developed the talent of making beautiful greeting cards. She dries flower petals and leaves of all shapes, sizes, and colors. She gets card stock and envelopes from a local printer. She places five or six dried petals or leaves on the cover of the card in a unique design and covers it with clear plastic adhesive film. It costs her about 10 cents for the card and the envelope. She sells her unique gifts for 75 cents each and donates the money to her church.

Last year, when our Cub Scout pack needed money for a Pinewood Derby track, I offered my bread-making skills. All of the boys went around their neighborhoods and took orders in advance, selling the bread at my customary prices. The Saturday we made the bread, they came over to help. Then they delivered their orders. Eight boys and I made about $200 in one day on the sale of 100 loaves of homemade bread.

These introductory comments notwithstanding, let's take a look at some of the things libraries do to make money.

ART FAIR

North Castle Library in Armonk, New York, (population 9,500), has an outdoor art show every year. They raise approximately $20,000 by hosting a juried show, which draws 200 exhibitors. The artists and the crafts people bring their wares for exhibit and sale. The event is supplemented with food booths, raffles, and donations at the gate. This annual event is run entirely by the Friends of the Library. Because it is an annual event, it draws a county-wide crowd. Over the years it has contributed regularly to the library for both building and equipment.

STREET FAIR

Joan Duke of Sedona, Arizona, reported that her library made $20,000 from a street fair organized by one of the board members. "It was one-day event. Everything was donated for the fair. Twenty booths selling plants, quilts, wood products, books, balloons, white elephant items, etc. We had a variety of entertainment throughout the day: musical groups, a gymnast, a storyteller. No one charged for their services, time, or material.

"The board member in charge had a committee of about a half dozen helpers. These people were all community members. But the board of trustees all worked on the fair, as did the library staff, and our 70-plus library volunteers. Community response was excellent."

ICE CREAM SOCIAL

In Ellis, Kansas, on the second Sunday in August you can count on homemade ice cream, cake and iced tea, and live entertainment in the park. The men make the ice cream, almost competing with each other for best ice cream of the day, though there is no judging or prizes. The women are the same about their cakes. They might spend $5 or $6 and an entire afternoon on their favorite cake. Everything sells for 50 cents a serving. They ask volunteers to donate cakes, ice cream, and tea. With a little advertising, everything falls into place. A blue grass group volunteers its talents. Some feel it is a lot of work for the money they make.

USED JEWELRY SALE

Another library has a used jewelry sale every year at the same time the downtown merchants have their annual sidewalk sales. About six months before the sale, the library advertises that it needs used jewelry for the sale, and people bring in stuff they don't want or need. The librarian has found pieces made of solid silver with turquoise that probably sold for $50 or more originally. It's all donated to the library, which puts these pieces in with the rest of the jewelry and sells them for 50 cents apiece. Bargain hunters love it, and the library makes several hundred dollars.

AUTHOR LUNCHEONS

The Friends of the Willcox, Arizona Public Library sponsor an annual author luncheon. They invite local authors to come and speak at a luncheon, which they arrange at a restaurant. Advertising is low-budget, using radio public service announcements and news releases. The visibility is worth as much as the money they raise. They sell tickets in advance and ask the authors to donate 30 percent of their profits from the books sold at the luncheon. They usually make less than $500 in a community of 3,800 people. It is a lot of work. The next time they do it, they plan to step up promotion and have the food catered at the community center. Sometimes they have the hassle of getting books in from the publishers and returning the ones they don't sell. The year my father, Walter Swan, appeared on the program that wasn't a problem. He was both author and publisher of his book, *"me n' Henry."*

The effort may not be worth the money raised, but those who come enjoy it, and it is good visibility for the library.

PANCAKE FEED

For more than 15 years the Noon Kiwanis Club in Great Bend, Kansas, has been perfecting its pancake supper. Ten years ago, they made $6,000 on their single fundraising event of the year. Most recently, they netted over $10,000, without increasing the price of their tickets. They must be doing something right.

They don't buy anything they can get donated. Everything from sausage to syrup, pancake mix to coffee. They contact local merchants and ask them to furnish the food products they need. Every member competes at selling tickets. They tell people, "The tickets are so cheap ($1.50), you don't even have to come." The winners get a steak dinner—all donated, of course.

They rent the gymnasium of the local Catholic church/school for the event and start serving at 11:00 a.m.. They serve pancakes, sausage, and coffee, tea, or orange drink. The serving line rivals lines at Disneyland in August. If you get there at the right time, you might be served in less than an hour.

Every member participates, doing everything from taking tickets to refilling coffee cups. All the food is served on plastic, so clean-up is easy and carry-out is a snap.

CHILDREN'S DINNER THEATER

In American Fork, Utah, they hold a children's dinner theater. As often as twice a year, the children and library staff make puppets and put on a show for family and friends. Families bring their own food from home, spread a quilt on the floor of the library, and have a picnic during the performance. The children are given favors by the Friends of the Library. Families buy a family ticket for the puppet show. The community gets a terrific social activity, and the library profits from admission charges.

LOCAL TRIVIA GAME

A library group in Glasco, Kansas, (population 710), teamed up with the free university, a local adult education group that needed money, too. Together they published a "Glasco Trivia Game." Townspeople submitted questions and answers. The library and the free university divided the work and split the profits.

GARDEN/HOME TOUR WITH BUFFET

Diane Slater, librarian in Liberal, Kansas, (population 16,000), raised $2,700 to renovate and remodel their building with a garden and home tour and a buffet dinner. They attracted a large number of donors.

On the down side, it was a "killer" for the cooks. They served 155 people with food costs of $3.70 per plate. But they made a comfortable profit. Diane warns, "Don't try to do all the work yourself—cater the food." She attributes their success to:

1. Planning the meal carefully.
2. Arranging to use the Petroleum Club kitchen and serving facility.
3. Finding volunteers to help prepare, cook, and serve the meal.
4. Finding a social organization willing to act as servers and clean up afterwards
5. Buying all supplies through restaurant suppliers.

She lists these problems:

1. Cooks worked an average of 48 hours in three days The librarian worked 52 hours.

2. The club's kitchen wasn't available until three hours before the meal was to be served.
3. Because the food was served buffet style, some people ate more than was expected, causing a shortage of some dishes.

CASHING PROMOTIONAL COUPONS

In Havre, Montana, (population 17,896), a coupon project brought in more than $30,000. Everyone in the community clipped and saved coupons. The PEO taped them on the products at the store, and people donated if they wished.

In Wisconsin, the Rhinelander District Library arranged with one grocery store to give five cents for every UPC label from Red and White products. Another store gave one percent before taxes on cash register receipts.

CONTACT CIVIC GROUPS

Afton Lefever of Cedar City, Utah, (population 12,500), contacted community service organizations and literary clubs by letter and in person, asking for a contribution to help pay for the Bicentennial Bookshelf they wanted in the library. She explained the importance of the project and soon had enough money.

When the Library Board in Delphos, Kansas, contacted the local Lions Club, they got more than they bargained for: they got a new library. Delphos is a struggling farm community of 570 people in north central Kansas. Funds for community projects usually come $100 or $200 at a time from soup suppers, pancake feeds, and quilt raffles. Raising enough money for a new library seemed almost out of reach to the board. The Lions Club's effort was gratifying indeed.

They secured a matching grant from Lions Club International Foundation and organized hundreds of volunteer hours to remodel an old bank, converting it to a modest library with a meeting room. The whole community pitched in with the Lions and their leaders.

BIG TIPS

In a "Tip Me Big" program, librarians serve as waiters at a fancy meal. They ask donors to tip them *big*. They make arrangements with the restaurant to reserve the place for the whole evening. They invite their rich friends and ask them to leave a big tip for the library.

JAILING CELEBRITIES

The Heart Fund is raising money by putting local celebrities in jail (with their permission of course) and asking each one to raise $100 bond. The fundraisers promise "a light lunch after which a 'hanging' judge will find you guilty of overeating."

RAFFLES

As part of the annual Woodstock library fair, they have large raffle with a trip as the first prize. It raises a lot of money for the library.

A library in Utah reported that they raffled baby quilts. They were let down because the money raised barely covered the cost of materials for the quilt, let alone the time involved. Selling handicrafts for the library was not successful. They caution other fundraisers who want to make something and sell/raffle it: "Don't try to sell something the people are inclined to make for themselves. Women in Utah are handicraft minded." Another point: Check local laws. The library discontinued the practice when they learned that raffles are illegal in Utah.

The Chamber of Commerce in a community of 500 people raffled a new car, selling the tickets for $20. They barely broke even after paying for the car. The car dealer made more money on the deal than the Chamber did.

READ-A-THON

Pat Heidrick, director of the library in Beloit, Kansas, (population 2,500), has a 24-hour read-a-thon every year. She schedules local citizens to come in and read for 15 minutes. They ask for donations of those who come to read and to listen.

Another way to handle it is to have children get pledges for so much for each page they read. Then have a library "lock-in" slumber party while the children read. The one to raise the most money wins a prize.

COOKBOOKS

This is a good money-maker. You gather recipes from all your friends, type them up on cards, and send them to a fundraising cookbook publisher. The fundraising variety cookbook is either a looseleaf notebook type or plastic comb-bound type. One publisher, Cookbooks by Morris Press, P.O. Box 1881 Kearney, Nebraska, charges according to the binding, the number of pages, and the number of copies you order. They often require an up-front commitment of cash. When the cookbooks arrive, volunteers go out and sell them. I know several libraries that have made a few thousand dollars from an $8 cookbook.

When the Elroy (Wisconsin) Public Library needed a photocopier, librarian Barbara DeLong put together a community cookbook. The library solicited ads from local businesses and solicited recipes from the community. They sold the cookbook for $5, netting over $1,295.

Barbara said, "We planned it so the cookbook arrived in early November for sale as Christmas presents. The cookbook cover featured the library as it appeared in 1908, with a short history of the library right at the beginning of the book."

SELL AN IDEA TO OTHER LIBRARIES

In 1988 the Great Bend Public Library prepared "Assignment Alert Packets" for distribution to local teachers. The purpose of the packet was to encourage teachers to notify the public library when a library assignment was imminent. It was such a success that it was offered to other libraries for $8. The librarian sent copies to professional journals and asked them to feature it. The library grossed over $3,500 in less than a year.

WINE TASTING

The winery sets up the wine tasting as an advertisement. You charge the guests for the opportunity to come and drink the wine free. It is often a big social event, but don't do it in a community where a predominant religion frowns on the use of alcoholic beverages. They may not picket the event, but they probably won't come, either.

DINNERS

The Arcade, New York Free Library (population 3,714) needed to purchase some computer furniture. They held a series of salad luncheons. The library staff, volunteers, and Friends of the library agreed to set a specific number of tables and provide a variety of salads. Tickets were sold by the same people. Selling out every time, they raised $1,000 at each luncheon.

The setting was quite elegant. Part of the library was the first floor of a former residence. They use the former living rooms and dining area for reading rooms, meeting rooms, and cultural activities. They suggest you check with other groups in the community. Don't conflict with some other organization's fundraiser.

PIGGYBACK ON SOMETHING ELSE

Carolyn Bessey from Manti, Utah, (population 2,500), reports selling canned pop with paper cups of ice, popcorn, caramel popcorn, apple pie, and ice cream in a booth at the town's Fourth of July celebration in the park. The ice cream went well on the Fourth of July. They held a pie baking contest to get the pies.

"It was a PR effort as well as a fundraiser. We were all dressed as pioneers. It was a lot of fun," Carolyn said.

Sheila Blume, the librarian in a new school/community library in Kensington, Kansas, (population 600), tells of an ice cream social held on the night of a softball game.

"We held it in the park across the street from the softball diamond when we knew a game was scheduled for that evening," said Sheila. "We asked for a donation to the library and received more than if we had charged 50 cents a dish for the ice cream."

Fundraisers for the McCracken, Kansas Public Library piggybacked on the town centennial celebration to publish a cookbook that netted $5,000.

RECYCLE JUNK CARS

Mark Cunningham was the chair of the fundraising committee for the Ellsworth, Kansas, library building fund. A local automobile dealer, he made arrangements with a scrap metal recycling firm to come to Ellsworth to pick up junk cars and haul them off for scrap metal. The proceeds—about $50 per car—went to the library building fund.

BINGO

Charities in Great Bend, Kansas, (population 17,000), can make $5,000 a year from bingo. They contract with the operators of the bingo hall for one night a week at a certain price. After paying the overhead, they keep the remaining proceeds. What about setting up your own bingo hall and operating it as a business?

CARNIVALS

Everyone has a good time at carnivals, especially the children. Carnivals not only provide an opportunity for social activities for families, but they make money in a unique way. They require a lot of work for the money you make, but they are a lot of fun. If you do a raffle get the prizes donated.

At age 16, my twin brother, Jerry, and I put together a 4-H carnival. We went all over town gathering refrigerator cartons to build the booths. We got club members to be in charge of individual booths. Club members also sold books of tickets with a chance on the door prize (which we had arranged for someone to donate). Everyone in the community came, and the 4-H club made more money than they had in years.

STYLE SHOW
In Barneveld, Wisconsin the public library is the beneficiary of the Woman's Club Annual fashion show and salad luncheon. They raise $700 each year in a town of 625 people.

CHILDREN'S BOOK FAIR
This is a ready-made money-making event for libraries. Most vendors will bring in their wares (paperback books) and set up the display for a week. The library makes a commission of between 20 and 40 percent. You do need a few volunteers, but it beats peddling candy door-to-door.

NEWSPAPER PLEA
R. Elaine Perry in Spearfish, South Dakota, (population 5,400), raised matching funds for books on the constitution with pleas for help in the local newspapers. They had more than enough money in a short time.

FINAL SUGGESTIONS
Here a few last ideas you can offer in a brainstorming session. Turn your group loose on these. They might come up with a winner.

- antique bazaar
- "artistic" hot dog sale
- attic auction
- battle of the bands
- beauty contest
- benefit dinner/dance
- car washes
- card parties
- catering service
- celebrity baseball game
- Christmas card or tree sales
- contracted special programs
- craft classes—find a sponsor and sell the crafts
- crafts boutique
- dollhouse show
- fishing tournaments
- flea market

- flower sales
- follies
- friends logo item sale
- garage sales
- golf tournaments
- handyman
- horseshoe pitching
- junior Friends workdays
- lectures, concerts
- luau
- plant boutique
- potlucks
- radio & TV station auctions
- recognitions
- rent-a-grandmother, grandfather or kid
- rental collections, video cassettes
- rodeos
- rummage sales
- speakers bureau
- sports tournaments
- street dances
- swap meets
- talent show
- testimonial dinner
- theater parties
- tours
- tractor pulls

SUMMARY

Although, as we have stressed, selling things to make money for your library can be more work than it is worth, the benefits of increased visibility and an expanded donor base may make the difference. When it comes to fundraising, you have to start somewhere. Make sure you're selling something the people in your community will buy. If you have a well-developed, generous constituency, solicit a donation rather than sell something.

12 AUCTIONS

Auctions are a great way to raise money for your library—when you do it right. Doing it right depends on your community and its patterns of giving.

Phil Grossardt, Executive Director of Development for the Barton County (Kansas) Community College Foundation, gives an insight into both sides of success. In 1979 the Foundation started a benefit auction. It was an exclusive affair—black tie and tails, etc. It later became a semi-formal affair. Tickets were $20, and the merchandise for auction was expensive. Only the elite came. The Foundation averaged $10,000 per auction. This modest effort appealed to a very special group of people.

In 1981 the oil crunch hit, adversely affecting the economy of Barton County. The big royalty checks stopped rolling in, and the big spenders stopped spending. For five years the annual auction went downhill, until the organizer announced that they were going to discontinue the auction altogether.

Enter Phil Grossardt. He said, "We can't have an exclusive air in a rural community. In order for our auction to succeed we need a fairly wide appeal. People need to feel that they belong." An exclusive affair might work in a larger setting, such as Boston or Dallas, but it didn't work in Great Bend, Kansas.

Phil Grossardt set about reorganizing the Foundation auction. After he convinced the board that a different format would work, he set a new course. His new goals were:

- To generate additional private funding for academic scholarships at BCCC through an auction format.
- To promote annual giving to the BCCC Foundation by sponsoring an event centered on a informal environment of fun and social interaction.
- To secure items of *quality* that people would be interested in bidding on—items that will sell for respectable amounts.
- To keep costs down through establishment of a policy preventing the Foundation from buying gifts to auction or paying for services related to the auction.

To achieve these goals he set the following objectives:

- Secure free (donated) radio and newspaper advertising to help promote the event.
- Move the auction to a larger location and to a Friday night to help draw a larger crowd.
- Lower ticket prices ($5 each) and sell tickets at the door (in addition to advance sales).

- Eliminate the dance and the expense of the band.
- Devise several new "fun" events to help generate interest and excitement.
- In revamping the format, ask local beverage distributors to provide free beer and pop. Ask local vendors to sell food/snacks on the premises.
- Maintain quality in all items auctioned.
- Limit silent auction to items valued at $100 and less. Live auction items should have a value of $100 or more.
- Mail invitations one month in advance and the official auction catalog one week in advance.

EVALUATION

In reviewing what went well, Phil offered the following:

- All sale items were donated.
- The auctioneer donated his services.
- Use of the building was donated, and there was plenty of room.
- Targeting gifts and donors by using the master wish list helped attract many nice gifts for the auction. (See Master Gift List on page 170.)
- One hundred items for the live auction seems to be the right amount. This depends on the auctioneer.
- The volunteers felt comfortable with the format.
- Everyone who came had a good time.
- Everyone is looking forward to next year.

Phil offers these suggestions to others:

- People think they are going to get a bargain at an auction. Play that angle up. Create an atmosphere of competition.
- You can't expect to get everything free. Sometimes you will have to pay for printing, use of the hall, janitor service, advertising, etc.
- Ask for donations and do not accept an item if the donor wants you to pay something for it. Even if it is a good deal.
- Cater to your audience. Try to secure the gifts they will bid on.
- Establish your criteria for giving up front.
- High-value reconditioned items may be all right. For example, a microwave or vacuum.
- Make a prospect list and ask volunteers to sign up for businesses they want to solicit. Have each volunteer make at least five calls.
- Take care of your donors. (Make a fuss over them.) A toaster this year may become a TV next year. If you give them lots of

whatever it is they are buying (a good feeling, recognition, a feeling of importance), they will buy more of it next year.
- Organize your auction well. Give people a job to do and let them do it.

Here are a few don'ts:

- Don't make it too exclusive.
- Don't schedule your auction on top of another community event.
- Don't spend too much money.
- Don't buy items to auction.
- Don't accept poor quality used items or junk.

ORGANIZATION

Someone always has to be in charge. That person is called an auction coordinator. He or she may have as many committee chairs as necessary. The Barton County Foundation has three auction coordinators and four committee chairs. Each one has certain responsibilities. Here is the job description Phil gave to his auction coordinators:

Auction Coordinators must:

- serve as community representative/liaisons in the promotion of the event
- provide overall support in planning efforts
- generate ideas for and carry out the securing of unique live auction items
- sell tickets and put up posters
- help with arrangements and set up the day prior to and actual day of the event.

Every successful auction has enough of the right items to generate enthusiasm. Volunteers ask for gifts from businesses to sell at auction. A master list of prospects and a wish list is the heart of the solicitation effort. This list is made up by the auction gift committee. It lists the names of prospective businesses with contact person and address. It has a column for desired items (suggestions only) and another column for volunteers to sign up as a solicitor to the business.

MASTER GIFT LIST

Prospect	Item Wished For	Volunteer's Name
A to Z Mini Storage Abraham Zlotski 1928 Wall Street.	One year's worth of free storage	_____
*Action Sporting Goods Bob Rose 1987 Main	Pair of jogging shoes	_____
*Action Video Robert Rabbit 243 North Broadway	One free video rental every month for a year	_____
*American Security Bank Harry Derr 98 South Main	$100 savings bond	_____
Andrew's Television Milton Berlin 123 North Main	VCR or portable TV	_____
Art Emporium Melissa Crockett 243 East First	Framing of one picture	_____
Audiovisual Electronics Bill Bixley 5654 Rock Island Road	In-dash AM/FM Cassette	_____
Bailey's Dry Cleaning Alan Bailey 4563 Rock Island Road	Free storage box for one year	_____
Becker Rental and Equipment Keith Becker 864 Grand Ave.	Charbroil gas grill	_____

Previous donor.

Benefit Auction
ORGANIZATION CHART

Source: Barton County Community College Foundation

```
                    ┌─────────────────────┐
                    │   Foundation Board  │
                    │     and Director    │
                    └─────────────────────┘
```

Auction Coordinator	Auction Coordinator	Auction Coordinator

Gifts Commitee	Ticket Sales	Food-Beverage-Set-up	Finance

Phil says, "Be specific. If you want a ten-speed bicycle, ask for a ten-speed bicycle. Otherwise, you might end up with a screwdriver." You can start high and work down, but it is difficult to move up once you have made your first request. If they won't give a ten-speed bike, maybe they will give a coaster wagon. If they don't want to give merchandise ask for a cash gift.

Phil urges his solicitors to "sell the joy of giving." People who give have to feel part of the cause, which in this case is money for scholarships for young people to go to college. You know best how to define the cause for your library.

Make up your own prospect and gift list based on this one. Sit down with your gift committee and your telephone directory. The chamber of commerce membership list is also a good source. Make a list of all the businesses in town and create a list of possible gifts for your solicitors. All prospects on the Master Gift List receive a letter one week before personal calls are made.

The problem with very small communities is that businesses are always being asked to contribute to local causes. Some proprietors resent it. If you can, expand your base of donors. One library wrote to famous Hollywood personalities and requested that they donate an item they had once used. They received several valuable items

AUCTION CATEGORIES
The BCCC Foundation auction has three categories of items in their auction.

Door prizes—valued under $20, given away at auction by ticket stub number.

Silent auction items—valued under $100.

Live auction items—valued over $100.

for their auction. If you can justify a benefit your library offers the next community or surrounding area, you can reach out to them for gifts.

You may have to resort to used items in order to have enough stuff to sell. If you do, make sure that you limit what you will take to quality items that people want to buy. Appliances that originally sold for $300 to $500 in good condition are good bets. Bicycles or exercise equipment in good working order are another. Quality furniture might sell, again if it's in good condition. Don't even consider used personal items, things that don't work, and junk. Remember that used items won't bring high prices. Your auction won't make as much money, but people will have a good time.

You need to decide whether or not to charge for admission. It is obviously a way to enhance the income for the library. Besides the proceeds from the auction, you will have the money from admission charges. This is pure profit unless you pay for refreshments that you give away inside. Many Friends groups hold an annual auction of quality merchandise; membership in the Friends of the library is the admission price. Membership in various Friends groups runs $5 to $25. If other people want to come to the auction, they can join the Friends group at the door.

You can make a lot of money selling tickets to people who do not plan to attend the auction. They consider it a donation. You can organize committees and canvass the whole town, selling tickets to your auction.

Your auction could become an excellent annual event. If you do it year after year, improving it as you learn from your experiences, people will look forward to it and want to be part of it. Every year hold a debriefing session with all of your workers. Ask three questions: What went well? What could we have done to improve it? What should we try next year to make it better? Write your answers down and refer to them next year when you plan for the next auction.

Keep track of what each merchant gives you for the auction. Base next year's solicitation on last year's gift. Try to move them to a higher level of giving. If a hardware store gave you an electric drill last year, try for two drills or a circular saw or a belt sander this year. If they say no, thank them for their gift and move on. Once a firm establishes a level of giving, it may be difficult to move them to a higher level, but don't stop trying.

Try for variety in the auction items you solicit. Three or four of the same items may drive down the price and makes the auction boring. Not everybody will want to bid on a ten-speed bike or a set of radial tires. If you have identical items, such as one free movie rental per month for a year, mix them up in the order of selling in the live auction.

Remember the tax write-off for an auction goes to the merchant who gave the gift, not to the person who bought it. The merchant can claim only the cost of the gift, not its selling price. Promote the tax benefit when you solicit the gift. Most companies can count it as a business expense or a charitable contribution. The person who buys the item receives merchandise in return for his purchase. He may look at it as a contribution to your cause, but he is really buying something. The buyer can claim a tax deduction if he pays more for the item than it would sell for in the store. For example: Sears sells a bike for $100. They donate the bike to the auction, and it is listed in the catalog for $100. If a bidder buys the bike for $150, he can claim $50 as a charitable deduction.

CREATING A CATALOG

Once all of the auction items are lined up, it is time to put a catalog together. This document merits your careful effort and attention. You use this document to attract people to the auction and create enthusiasm to buy. The auction is where you make your money. A gift valued at $500 that sells for $300 at auction only nets your library $300. The job of the auction catalog is to help you sell each item for as much as possible.

You create interest in each item by the way you describe it. This is your opportunity to tap a community resource. Find someone who is adept with words. Ask them to do a clever 25-word description of each item. Be sure to give each item a number and include the donor's name or business and the estimated retail value.

The first page of the catalog should include a welcome to the bidders and overall instruction on how the auction will work. Your job here is to explain the rules of the game. Some people have never been to an auction before. They need to feel comfortable.

You might also want to make a statement about the purpose of the auction. Remind your bidders that this auction benefits your library. Mention the benefits and tell them that if they purchase an item for more than the estimated retail price, the difference is tax-deductible. Your catalog gives you a chance to recognize your

WELCOME to the 11th Annual Benefit Auction!

General Information

1. All bidders must have a bidder number.
2. Payment may be made after an item is purchased, or if bidding on several items, immediately following the auction.
3. Payment must be made with cash or check at the designated cashier's table the night of the auction.
4. Make checks payable to the Barton County Community College Foundation.
5. Please claim your purchases promptly after the live auction by presenting your paid receipt. Please remove all items purchased the night of the auction.
6. All sales are final. No refunds or exchanges will be made.
7. Unless otherwise specified, all auction items and services must be used by December 31, 1989.
8. Arrangements to redeem service items must be made with the individual contributor and should be done at the earliest convenience.

Silent Bid Rules

1. Silent bidding begins at 6:30 p.m.
2. Each item on display or described in the Silent Bid area has its own bidding sheet. To place a bid, write your bidder number and amount of bid on the sheet.
3. Increase the previous bid by as much as you like, but each new bid must be raised by **at least** one dollar.
4. Check on your bid frequently. It may be topped at any time!
5. Bid on any Silent Bid item as many times as you wish.
6. Silent bidding will close at 9:00 p.m.
7. The last person whose bid appears on the sheet when silent bidding concludes purchases the item.
8. Please pay for all Silent Bid winnings at the cashier's table.

Live Auction Rules

1. All live bidders must have a bidder number.
2. The Live Auction will begin at approximately 8 p.m. and will continue without interruption until all items are sold.
3. The successful bidder's number will be recorded by the cashier.
4. The auctioneer will act as final authority on all sales.

Door Prizes

1. Your admission ticket could enable you to win valuable prizes.
2. Tickets will be torn in half and placed in a container. HANG ONTO YOUR TICKET STUB! Numbers will be drawn randomly. If the number on your stub matches the one drawn, you win!
3. Once inside, additional tickets will be sold for one dollar. Increase your chances of winning by buying several tickets!
4. Extra chances will be on sale at the cashier's table.
5. YOU MUST BE PRESENT TO WIN!

Dress

The purpose of this auction is to raise money for academic scholarships and to have fun in the process. Dress casual...wear your jeans...above all, be comfortable. Enjoying yourself is most important!

workers and donors. Make sure everyone who volunteered or made a contribution is named in the catalog.

About three months before the auction, one of the BCCC Foundation Auction coordinators called and asked me to make some bread for the auction. I had already decided to retire from the bread business, so I couldn't benefit from the advertising or prospect for better bread business. I said yes because I wanted to be part of other organizations' fundraising efforts. I am also a sucker for recognition. It was great to see my name in the catalog and to think that others had recognized me for my excellent bread. It was even more gratifying to watch 12 loaves of bread sell for $40—a 50 percent premium.

People like to be associated with a successful project. Make your catalog look as professional as you can make it—even if you have to spend a little money to have it typeset. With desk-top publishing readily available, you can find the resources to produce an attractive catalog.

Make it as good as you can. No one wants to be associated with a loser. If your catalog looks like you zapped it off with a dirty typewriter at the last minute, people will wonder if you mean business. Next year they will think twice about supporting your auction.

If your auction is a one-time effort, or if your are selling a lot of used stuff, it may not be worth a catalog. Nonetheless, a hand bill listing the items for sale is the bare minimum. The way you make money at an auction is to have a crowd of people to bid on the items for sale. The way to insure a large crowd is to have lots of good stuff and advertise it. A week before the auction, the BCCC Foundation sent everyone on their mailing list a copy of the catalog.

Good advertising? You bet!

The expense of printing the catalog was underwritten by the college. You may not be that lucky, but you can have someone set the type for you. If you have a copier that will print 11" X 17" paper, try that format, printed on both sides and fold the sheets into a booklet. It will look nicer and be easier to use than if you staple a bunch of pages together.

A week before the auction the BCCC Foundation sent a free ticket to each donor. It insured a large crowd and created goodwill among the donors. But the coordinators are taking a second look at the idea. The value of the tickets was over $1,000. Was the donor goodwill worth it? Would they have bought tickets anyway? Who knows? This is a decision you will have to make when you organize your auction.

LIVE BID

LA1 PIZZA PARTY

Enjoy one large specialty pizza each month for a year! Choose Supreme, Meat Lovers, Cheese Lovers, Taco, BBQ or any three topping pizza. Offer good beginning in May of '89 and lasting through April of 1990.
Value: $150   Donor: Jim Ellis
                                         Pizza Huts of Barton Co.

LA2 LOOK YOUR BEST

Let the pros at Suburban Dry Cleaning in Great Bend care for your clothes. Save $150 with this special gift certificate. Your clothes will look better and last longer with Suburban!
Value: $150   Donor: Ed Herres
                                 Suburban Dry Cleaning, Great Bend

LA3 MOVIE MADNESS

Go nuts and rent all your favorite movies. Razzle Dazzle Video gives you one movie video rental per week for one full year! Offer good Mondays through Thursdays only.
Value: $156   Donor: Joe Wilson
                                    Razzle Dazzle Video

LA4 DOOR TO DOOR

Time to replace that old storm door? Well, here's your chance. With full-length glass, this energy saving storm door by Croft measures three feet by 6 feet. Comes in white and features tempered glass for your family's safety.
Value: $120   Donor: Vince Fries
                                 Home Lumber & Supply

LA5 COOK WITH POWER

Only Amana makes the famous "Radarange," microwave oven. This one features electronic readout time and temperature plus 10 cookmatic settings to make your kitchen chores a snap!
Value: $180   Donor: Jay Miller
                              Home Appliance Company

LA6 "OH CHRISTMAS TREE, OH CHRISTMAS TREE!"

Christmas 1989 will be here before you know it. Get a jump on the season now with this new white flocked artificial tree. Six and one half feet tall, with stand.
Value: $200   Donor: Dale and Jane Engleman,
                                         Great Bend

LA7 BED N' BREAKFAST FOR TWO

Salina's beautiful Holidome is the site for this bed and breakfast special. You and a guest will stay in one of the hotel's suites on the Saturday night of your choice, and then enjoy the Holidome's lavish Sunday brunch the following morning. (Reservations required).
Value: $125   Donor: Harper Corporation-
                          Holiday Inns of Great Bend & Salina

LA8 AWARD-WINNING WATERCOLORIST-

And award-winning artist - BCCC's own art instructor, Steve Dudek, is back with another one of his original paintings. This framed watercolor will add the perfect touch to the decor of your home or office. Would make a great gift for a special friend, too!
Value: Tremendous   Donor: Steve Dudek
                                  BCCC Art Instructor

LA9 IT'S FOR YOU

Don't miss anymore calls with Southwestern Bell's Feature Phone and Answering Machine. Beeperless remote, two-way record, voice-activated (VOX) recording, call screening, and flashing message counter. Switchable for pulse or tone systems.
Value: $150   Donor: David Toburen
                            Water's True Value Hdwr.

LA10 HUNTING FOR A DAY AT FORT DUCK

Dr. Rick Krause will take up to two people on a special one day hunt at Fort Duck, a private hunting area near the Quivira Wildlife Refuge. Ducks, geese, quail or pheasants await you. So does a warm, crackling fire afterwards in the Fort Duck clubhouse. For the 89/90 hunting season!
Value: Very good   Donor: Dr. Rick Krause

Setting the date

You want as many people as possible to come to your auction. The best way to insure that is to pick a day and time attractive to most people. Friday night, Saturday, or Sunday are your best bets. A caution is offered by Lorraine B. Cederholm from Princeton Public Library: "Have your auction on Saturday. We held ours on Sunday after all the tourists went home." If you rely on tourists for support of your auction, don't hold it on the day they head for home, especially in the afternoon. My preference is Friday night. Try not to schedule it in conflict with something that is already scheduled. If your auction is an annual event, hold it the same day of the month every year; e.g. the last Friday night in March. After a while, other organizations in town will know that you hold your auction then and avoid that date. If you are just starting, select your date several months in advance and publicize it. Remember, the purpose of setting the date for your auction is to insure a good crowd. It may take time, but if you keep at it and offer a good time to everyone, it won't be long before you will have a successful event.

Before the auction

The week before the auction, the coordinators should call the donors to remind them of their commitment and make arrangements either to pick up the gifts or have the donor deliver them. Check with owners of the hall where the auction will be held to make sure that heating, lighting, and cooling are ready for your event. Check with the custodial help to make sure that the place will be clean and ready for your set-up of tables and chairs. Check with those who are responsible for the physical set-up. Make sure your auctioneer has everything he needs. Check on bidder cards, name badges, and last-minute printing. You don't want to start the auction without bidder cards. Check on refreshments. If you promised free beer, make sure it is there and that you are in compliance with pertinent laws.

In general, check with everybody about everything. Make sure of all commitments. Communication is a key to a smoothly-running event. If you have everything set up the way you want it and fail to confirm it at the last minute, you will run into a snag. Someone will have forgotten something. Or someone will assume that something is covered when it hasn't been. Taking care of last minute details is essential. Check and double check them.

At the auction try to relax and let things flow as they will. If things go wrong, don't fret. Go to Plan B or Plan C, if necessary. Be prepared for any contingencies.

Try to be like the immigrant who came to America around the turn of the century and hired on as a farm worker in Minnesota. He spoke very little English, but he had a standard answer for each of his employer's questions. When asked if he knew how to milk cows, he answered, "I sleep when the wind blows." When asked if he could care for horses, he said, "I sleep when the wind blows." What about laying in hay or fixing the barn? The answer was always the same: "I sleep when the wind blows."

One evening a terrible storm came up. The farmer went looking for his hired hand and found him fast asleep in his room. The farmer went to check on his horses and cattle and barn. Everything had been readied for the storm. The horses were in their stalls with plenty of water and fodder. The cows were in their shelter with plenty of feed. There were no loose doors or boards in the barn. The hired hand had indeed taken care of everything before the wind blew. Now he was asleep.

The farmer went in and woke up the hired hand and asked why he was asleep. He said, "I told you: I sleep when the wind blows."

If you have done all you can to prepare for your auction and the wind blows, let it. It is too late to try to fix anything. The best you can do to salvage anything is let it happen as though you had planned it that way. Your attitude should be: "We will fix it next year."

A PLANNING TIME LINE

One year before auction: Review previous auction with planning committee. Ask: What went well? What could we have done to improve it? What should we try next year to make it better?

Six months before auction: Select and recruit auction coordinators.

Five months before auction:

> Select committee chairs.
> Begin monthly meetings with auction coordinators.
> Discuss previous auction and plans for improvement.
> Decide on the date and time.
> Decide on the location.
> Assign someone to make necessary contacts to secure commitment for the location.

Decide on an auctioneer.

Assign someone to confirm date with him or her. Remember, if last year's auctioneer did a good job and has volunteered for next year, repeat your invitation. Auctioneers are show people. They like to perform. Don't hurt their feelings by asking someone else, unless you have a very good reason.

Decide on a format for auction: silent bid, door prizes, or live auction.

Review donor list:

Add names for new businesses or prospects.

Delete names if necessary.

Review volunteer list:

Assign them to committees.

Assign auction coordinators to contact returning committee members and recruit new members.

Four months before auction:

Review all plans.

Confirm date and contract for the building.

Confirm arrangement with the auctioneer.

Confirm committee assignments.

Secure tentative commitments from food and beverage suppliers.

Review final master list of donors and wished for gifts.

Make arrangements for printing. The lead time for most print shops is three to six weeks. For big jobs it may be longer. Tell your printer what you plan to do and ask for a block of time about two weeks before the auction. The printer will need to know how many pages you will have, how many copies of the document you will need, what paper stock you want, and whether type will need to be set.

Have volunteers sign up to contact businesses for auction items.

Three months before auction:

Train volunteers to solicit gifts. Tell them to be specific. If you want a ten-speed bicycle, ask for one. If the prospective donor won't give that, ask for something else. If they won't give an item for the auction, ask for a cash contribution. Not all contacts have to be made in person, though it is preferable. Items for the silent bid or door prizes may be solicited over the telephone, but you will do far better if you can meet personally with each prospective donor.

Have them begin soliciting gifts.
Have tickets printed.

Three months before auction:

Review all plans.
Continue gift solicitation.
Meet with gift soliciting committee. Praise progress and encourage.
Recruit ticket selling committee.
Block out the auction catalog.

Two months before auction:

Review all plans.
Train the ticket-selling committee.
Begin selling tickets.
Meet with gifts committee. Have them check with donors for the final copy in auction catalog.
Check on the building, physical arrangements, etc.
Check again with auctioneer. Find out if he or she needs anything.
Check with printer to make sure that paper has been ordered and that production time has been scheduled.
Arrange for food and beverage for the event.

One month before the auction:

Begin meeting with coordinators weekly.
Review all plans.
Meet with ticket sales committee, praise progress. Answer questions.
Give final copy for the auction catalog to printer.

Three weeks before auction:

Meet with coordinators to review all plans.
Check on details.
Make contingency plans for possible problems.

Two weeks before auction:

Meet with ticket sellers. Reassign areas if necessary.
Meet with coordinators. Have them reconfirm all donations for auction and give instructions for having the merchandise delivered to the place of the auction just before the event.

Check on auction catalogs. Pick them up when ready.
Check with the auctioneer.
Check on physical facilities: building, table, chairs.

One week before the auction:

Meet with ticket sellers. Encourage them for one last push.
Mail catalogs to donors.
Mail catalogs to those who have contributed before.
Check on bidders badges.
Confirm concessions.

One day before the auction:

Visit auction site. Check on physical arrangements.
Make sure food area is ready for concessions.
Meet with volunteers who will run the auction.
  Check on details.
  Make specific assignments.
  Review all plans.
  Turn on heating or air conditioning. It could take a day to
    bring the building to a comfortable temperature.

The day of the auction:

Take care of contingencies as they occur.
Relax and enjoy yourself. Let things happen as you planned
  them.

The Monday after the auction:

Meet with auction community for a debriefing session.
  Take them to lunch, if possible.
  Tell everyone how much money you made.
  Celebrate.
  Discuss plans for next year.

One caution: You can lose the immediacy of the event by starting your planning too far in advance. It is better to work against a fairly tight timeframe. Most people perform better when they have a short deadline.

This planning time line can be used for any special event. You simply make a list of what needs to be done and who is going to do it, and then plug it into a calendar. It is wise to schedule a year's worth of monthly meetings with the volunteers 12 months before the event. Every meeting becomes a time for goal setting.

SUMMARY

Benefit auctions give people a chance to support a worthy cause, socialize, have a good time, and get something for their money. It is a great way to involve the entire community in a variety of ways. Merchants donate goods from their stores. Purchasers receive something for their money. Ticket purchasers donate to the fund and have a good time if they go to the auction. It is good way to raise money in a small community.

13 USED BOOK SALES

Making big dollars from a book sale requires going into it in a big way. It means a lot of hard work. You will have to recruit plenty of volunteers and solicit tons of books from the community. If you expect to make money from a book sale by weeding your collection and selling your worn-out, dog-eared books, forget it. The money you make won't be worth the effort. Think big and involve everyone who will volunteer. Book lovers enjoy handling and rummaging through old books. A book sale is a ready-made activity for the Friends of the library. Why not turn your sale over to them? It's fun and good publicity, too. It can also be a great membership recruiting tool.

A book sale is also a community service. It's next to impossible for some people to throw a book away, and most people have accumulated books they don't want any more. The sale is a great excuse to clean out the attic and bookshelves and to recycle books without destroying them. Books are like friends; we have emotional ties to them. We prefer to give them to someone who will enjoy them than to cart them out with the trash.

You may be doing someone a big favor by offering book ownership to those on limited incomes. Children, foreign students, and senior citizens are often beneficiaries of book sales.

A book sale is a low-overhead project. Your inventory is free; your expenses are low; and you can realize about $4 for every volunteer hour you spend on the book sale.

Of course the library always gets "first dibs" on any books that come in from the public. You can fill in missing periodicals, restock the paperback racks, and fill in a special collection. The Lawrence (Kansas) Public Library adds to its extensive hymn book collection from books destined for the used book sale. Most libraries accept gifts with the understanding that books donated to the library but not used in the collection will go to the book sale.

EARLY CONSIDERATIONS

If you want to try a book sale, make these decisions early:

When? By itself, or piggybacked with another event, such as a craft day, art guild show, sidewalk sale, etc?

How long? One day? A week? A single day book sale limits the public's access to you. Two days is a minimum. A week is better. Do you have the staff to run it for a week?

Where? Where can you hold the sale? Will you have to pay rent? Supply your own tables? Will you have adequate time beforehand to set up and afterwards to clear out? Will you be accessible? (You will also need to consider where to prepare for the sale, because sorting donations, pricing, storing boxes of books, etc. takes lots of room.) If your library is considering a new building it may be too crowded to store book sale books.

Who will help you? You will need book handlers to sort and price, publicity people to solicit donations and promote the sale. You will also need strong arms and backs for hauling boxes and setting up tables, and cashiers for the sale itself.

What? Will you limit donations to books or accept a variety of items? Besides books, you can ask for and sell magazines, records, tapes, art prints, sewing patterns, maps, games, and puzzles. If your space is limited, you may have to be more selective. But never assume that there isn't a market for particular item or category. You will be surprised at what people will buy.

GETTING THE BOOKS

Once you have made the decision to hold a book sale, the next step is to get some books to sell. Write a story for the local newspaper about the sale, telling how to donate books. It will get you started. You might also try posters around town. A classified ad in with the sale notices might bring in some garage sale left-overs. Most newspapers give a garage sale sign to garage sale advertisers. Why not try offering large grocery sacks to the newspaper to give to garage sale advertisers? You could write "Books for the Library Sale" on the bags. When their sale is over, they can put their books in the sack and bring them to the library.

Make up a flyer telling what you will accept (books, magazines, records, prints, sheet music, patterns, tapes, etc.) and where to bring the the stuff. Mention that the donation is tax-deductible as a charitable contribution. Friends who go to garage sales could hand them to the sellers as they go around. Whatever you use, make it clear how to get the books to you.

Everyone who accepts donations has to have a receipt form to give the donor for income tax purposes. By the way, when you issue a receipt, do not place a dollar value on the donation. The IRS says that the valuation is the responsibility of the donor. You are best off issuing a receipt that simply gives the number of hardback books and the number of paperbacks. You may agree to the value the donor puts on the books and note it on the receipt. Don't forget to say thank you and put their names on your donor list.

In your publicity, stress the following: what you will accept; how to get it to you; that it is a tax deductible donation; and that all proceeds will be used to benefit the library.

If you decide to include discarded books from the library collection, make sure you can do it legally. If it is all right, mark the books with a big (one-inch-high letters) stamp, *"No Longer the Property of (name) Public Library"* in several places. The last thing you want, after the library staff has gone to the trouble of withdrawing the book from the shelves and pulling the cards from the card catalog, is to have the book find its way back into the library by mistake.

SORTING AND PRICING

Sorting and pricing is the next big job. If your book sale becomes an annual event, bringing in $10,000 to $30,000, sorting and pricing will go on year-round. The success of your book sale will depend on the amount of sorting and organizing you do. Yes, people do like to browse and find hidden treasures, but with 20,000 to 30,000 books to look through, they need help. They may not have enough time or patience to keep searching. Many people will come to a book sale looking for a specific title, author, or subject. They will usually find things to buy if you make it easy for them. Small sales (2,000 books or less) may not require many categories. Try separating the paperbacks into westerns, romances, children's books, nonfiction, and novels. Do the same for the hardbacks. Try organizing the hardback nonfiction into the ten Dewey Decimal classes. Make a special display for science fiction, westerns, and children's materials; they always sell out.

After your first sale or two, you will begin to sense the needs of your community. This will be your guide for future sales.

You will receive some things you can't sell in the regular sale. Lawrence Public Library has boxes labeled "almost free." They toss books in terrible condition (covers falling off, pages loose, wet, and warped), giveaways, and out-of-date almanacs into these boxes. Boxes are put in the parking lot during the sale. A sign advertises: "Take what you want. Pay what it's worth to you." They make about $20 a year from these books.

More importantly, eliminating the really unsightly and out-of-date items from the tables and shelves makes the rest of the sale more attractive.

You may also find some valuable books. You will want to handle them separately. Lawrence, Kansas, librarians put aside books on Kansas or books by state authors. You can display them in a special manner and charge more for them. You may want to catch and put aside almost-new books that still have their jackets and appear to never have been read. First editions of famous authors, books autographed by the author, or anything that looks special to you—all can claim a premium price. You want to make it as easy as possible for your buyers to find what they want. A good used book sale could rival a quality second-hand book store for quality merchandise.

SUCCESS OR FAILURE

Pricing is the key to the success of your book sale. Charge too much, and you could be stuck with books that didn't sell. Charge too little, and your profits will suffer. Your goal is to make as much money as possible while moving as many books as you can. It all depends on your community, the books they give you, and their attitude toward used book sales. It may take several years to educate them.

The people in Lawrence, Kansas, offer the following ideas:

- If a customer really wants a book, she will buy it as readily for a dollar as for a nickel. If she doesn't want it, she won't take it if it's free.
- Customers adjust their thinking to whatever price range you establish. If most books are five cents, a book for 25 cents becomes something to think about twice. If most books are $1, a 50-cent book is a bargain.
- A book valued at $20 by a dealer won't sell for 20 cents unless someone who wants it comes to your sale.
- Small price increments are usually meaningless and make life harder for book sale workers. What is the difference between a 35-cent book and a 40-cent book? Try pricing everything in 25-cent or 50-cent increments.

Whatever you decide, try to make it easy for the pricers and the cashiers. You will make it easy for your customers too. Every book should have a price clearly marked in it. You might try large round dots and color code them. For example, books with red dots sell for 50 cents; books with blue dots sell for 75 cents; and books with white dots sell for $1. Pricing will vary according to your community and how well your book sale is received.

If your sale runs over several days, you can have a half-price sale on the last day. It will bring out the bargain hunters and gives people a second chance to buy something. During the final hour you might even offer books for a "buck a bag."

Decide for yourself if you want to haggle over price. I don't recommend it. If your sale lasts for several days, your books will have many chances to sell. Even if identical titles have different prices, just say, "We are all volunteers. We make mistakes." But always stand by the price as marked. If they still want to haggle, tell them to come back on the last day of the sale when everything will be half price. Some book sales sell by the pound. It sounds like a bargain hunter's paradise. Just make sure you have a good scale.

If you have difficulty deciding how much to charge, visit a local book dealer and see what he is charging. Your prices will have to be a little lower. Remember, people are looking for a bargain when they come to your book sale.

In general, remember to keep your system simple—easy for you to price, easy for customers and cashiers to decipher. Don't undervalue what you have. You are doing this to make money for the library. Be friendly but firm on the policy you establish on bargaining. After the sale, make notes about what sold well, what comments you heard about prices, and ways you might minimize your work and maximize your profit.

You don't have to be in a large town to make money from a used-book sale. Joan Tripp, librarian in Cooperstown, New York, (population 2,500) said the library makes about $2,000 each year with their Fourth of July book sale. People bring in books all year and the sale is a huge financial success.

PUBLIC RELATIONS

The public relations value of a book sale is immeasurable. It is truly a win-win situation. The donor gets rid of unwanted books. The buyer gets a bargain. The library gets a few books to add to its collection. The Friends get a lot of visibility (and new members, too, if they sell memberships at the book sale). The library benefits from the fundraising effort. And the whole town feels good about it.

SUMMARY

Book sales in college towns seem to be more successful because of the generally higher education level of the residents. Professors and

PLANNING WORKSHEET

Once you decide to hold a book sale, you will have to answer these questions before you can move ahead:

1. Who will be in charge?

2. What committees will we have? (Publicity, sorting, pricing, hauling, set up, take down, recruiting volunteers, securing books, etc.)

3. Who will head each of these committees?

4. When will we have it? (Spring, summer, or fall? In conjunction with something else?)

5. Where will we have it? (At the library? Indoors or outdoors?)

6. Where will we store the books before the book sale?

7. How will we display them? (Shelves, tables, boxes?)

8. How will we advertise to get books?

9. How will we advertise to get customers for the sale?

10. What will we accept as donations?

11. How will we handle thank you notes and receipts?

12. What will our price range be?

students are good customer for bargain books. They also tend to buy more books at regular prices, which they donate to the library book sale.

Libraries in very small communities may have discouragingly low profits from a book sale—either because they didn't have enough good books to sell or because the prices were too high or too low. Their community may not have been ready to pay a dollar per book, even for the good stuff. It may take several annual used book sales to build the expectations high enough to have a financially successful book sale.

Sometimes a librarian will weed the collection and offer the withdrawn books to the patrons for 25 cents each. This is hardly a book sale. It might make a few people feel better about weeding the collection because they are not actually throwing the book away— just recycling it, probably for the fiftieth time. I think books that have served their usefulness in a library should be respectfully disposed of in the trash. Let's not confuse the disposing of discarded books with a book sale.

14 FRIENDS AND FOUNDATIONS

Having a Friends of the library group and having your own foundation can provide your library with a steady source of income. Friends form a solid advocacy group that can increase the library's visibility. They can also be a formidable fundraising group. Friends have traditionally raised funds for projects or acquisitions in excess of the general library budget. A library foundation is a legally established, nonprofit organization formed for the purpose of receiving charitable gifts for the library. It is organized to become qualified as a 501 (c) (3) tax exempt entity. If a fundraising effort by the library is offset by a reduction in tax support, a foundation or a Friends group is a must. These are the only ways to protect donations that might come to the library, short of obtaining an agreement from the governing body to let you keep the money you raise without reducing tax support.

Melba Herman, Librarian at McCook, Nebraska, says, "Our library foundation sponsors the book sale and buys things for the library. Otherwise, we would have to turn the money over to the city to deposit in our fund to be budgeted."

The Ellis (Kansas) Library Friends (ELFS) have an ice cream social in the park every August. They sell memberships in the Friends group at the same time. The event expands Friends membership and brings the community together for a lot of fun just before the children go back to school.

BENEFITS OF A FRIENDS GROUP
The benefits of organizing a Friends group are not limited to fundraising. Here are a few other assets the Friends can bring to your library:

- volunteer service
- help with passage of a bond issue or tax referendum
- lobbying the legislature or city government
- public relations
- programming for the library
- a focal point for community support of the library.

Make sure you want a Friends group before you organize one. There is no more powerful benefit for your library than an active, well-directed Friends group. When the goals of the Friends coincide with the goals of the library, everything you set your hand to will succeed. However, it is essential that Friends cooperate with the library director and the board of trustees, but interfere with neither. Because of the independent nature of a Friends group, they can often undertake projects that far exceed the scope of trustees or staff. Library directors and boards may begin to count on the Friends as a source of regular funding—possibly as a substitute for adequate tax support. Generally, Friends like to see their money pay for high-visibility items in the library, such as art work, a speaker system, or chairs in the community room. It is a way of promoting membership. Fixing a leak in the basement is important, though it probably will not make the Friends "top ten list." The library board, director, and Friends need to work together to set priorities and define roles for the good of the library.

Once Friends are organized, put them to work right away. In the fall of 1980 we organized the Friends of the Great Bend Public Library. Immediately, we started a campaign to pass a tax referendum. Everyone worked hard and felt good when we won passage by 62 percent of the vote. Afterwards, interest dwindled and the Friends leadership found other interests. We had not kept them busy. Interest picked up again in 1988, when we went for another mill levy increase. Keep your Friends involved, and they will be a powerful force for the good of your library.

To recap: Cooperation and mutual goals are essential. None of the three entities should feel threatened by another. Each has a most important part to play in success for a library. Like the library, Friends need to have both long-range and short-range goals in order to keep active and moving forward.

FRIENDS AS FUNDRAISERS

Friends are valuable fundraisers. About half of the librarians who responded to my survey said that Friends were responsible for all library fundraising in their community. They are a ready-made fundraising committee for a major fund drive. Most of them viewed fundraising as part of the job when they "hired on." They expect to give and they expect to get others to give. They like to work for the library because they enjoy the benefits of the library.

If you have a Friends group whose interest is waning, try one or more of the following:

- Meet with those who are active and start a planning process to increase membership by 50 percent.
- Meet with those who are active and ask them to help the library review its mission, goals and objectives.
- Do a survey of all active Friends and ask them to list ideas for revitalizing the group.
- Ask them to help with a major public relations push.
- Start a literacy program and ask them to volunteer to be reading tutors.

- Develop a library "wish list" and challenge the Friends to raise the money to buy something from the list.
- Make plans for a colossal book sale and ask the Friends to be in charge.
- Brainstorm with them.

ORGANIZING A FRIENDS GROUP

Start with these steps:

1. Invite a few regular patrons of the library to come to the library. Tell them you would like to organize a Friends group.
2. Develop a tentative agenda for the first meeting.
3. Brainstorm for a list of people to invite to the organizational meeting.
4. Set the date for the first meeting (about a month in advance).
5. Send invitation letters to those on the list and explain the purpose of the meeting.

At the meeting:

1. Have the library director or the library board president conduct the meeting.
2. Outline that the goal of the meeting is to determine if there is enough interest in the community to organize a Friends of the library group.
3. Have an outside expert talk about what Friends do, the benefits to the library of a Friends group, and the benefits to individuals.
4. Have the library director outline two or three possible projects for the Friends and what might be expected of those who join the Friends.
5. Ask the group if there is enough interest to organize.
6. Elect a temporary president.
7. Appoint a nominating committee.
8. Appoint a constitution and by-laws committee and give them a charge to bring proposed constitution and by-laws to the next meeting.

9. Set the next meeting date.
10. Adjourn.

Meet with the committee to help draft by-laws. Have resource documents available. At the organizational meeting:

1. The temporary chair conducts.
2. Receive the report of the constitution and by-laws committee (copies for everyone).
3. Discuss and approve constitution and by-laws.
4. Receive the report of nominating committee.
5. Elect officers.
6. Receive a report from library director (plans and projects).
7. Appoint a membership committee.
8. Appoint projects committee.
9. Appoint a publicity committee.
10. Appoint committee to seek official recognition of the group from the state and to seek IRS 501 (c) (3) designation.
11. Adjourn.

This outline will help you get started. If you are looking for help from the Friends for a fundraising campaign, organize and put them to work. More on the subject can be found in *Friends of the Library Handbook* by Jean A. Ashfield and *Friends of Libraries Sourcebook*, edited by Sandy Dolnick.

Once you decide to organize, a seemingly formidable task is to write the constitution and by-laws. Fortunately, many sample documents are available. Here is one I have used. (The names have been changed.)

SAMPLE CONSTITUTION

ARTICLE I - NAME
The name of this organization shall be Friends of the Happy Hollow Public Library.

ARTICLE II - PURPOSE
The purposes of this organization are as follows:
(A) To maintain an association of persons interested in the Happy Hollow Public Library.
(B) To promote and stimulate the use of the library's resources and services.

(C) To make the public aware of the Friends of the Happy Hollow Public Library and the services they perform.

(D) To encourage and receive gifts and bequests to the library.

(E) To support and cooperate with the library in developing library services and facilities in the community.

(F) The purposes of the organization shall be limited to charitable and educational purposes within the meaning of Section 501 (c) (3) of the Internal Revenue Code.

No substantial part of the organization's activities shall involve attempts to influence legislation except as allowed under the provisions of Section 501 (h) of the Internal Revenue Code. The organization shall not carry on propaganda or intervene in any political campaign (including the publishing or distributing of statements) on behalf of any candidate for public office.

The organization shall not carry on any other activities not permitted to be carried on by:

(1) an organization exempt from Federal Income Tax under Section 501 (c) (3) of the Internal Revenue Code of 1954 (or the corresponding provisions of any future United States Internal Revenue Law);

(2) an organization, contributions to which are deductible under Section 170 (c) (2) of the Internal Revenue Code of 1954 (or the corresponding provisions of any future United States Internal Revenue Law).

ARTICLE III - MEMBERSHIP

Section 1: Membership of this organization shall be open to all persons interested in the library.

Section 2: Each membership shall be entitled to one vote. A family membership entitles each member of the family to one vote.

Section 3: The membership shall have the option to sponsor a Junior Friends group involving young people up to the age of eighteen.

ARTICLE IV - OFFICERS AND ELECTION

Section 1: The officers of the organization shall be vested in a Board of Directors which shall consist of three (3) Directors and a President, Vice President, Treasurer, and Secretary.

Section 2: Terms of Office

(A) All officers shall be elected for a one-year term.

(B) The election of officers and directors shall be held at the annual meeting, and they shall assume the duties of that officer immediately following election. Officers and directors shall be elected by a majority vote of those present at the annual meeting.

Section 3: Officers and directors shall be nominated by a nominating committee appointed by the president with the consent of the Board of Directors, such nominating committee to consist of one member of the Board of Directors and two persons appointed from the membership at large. The nominating committee shall not nominate any person who does not consent to such nomination. Nominations shall be submitted to the membership in writing at least two weeks prior to the annual meeting. Additional nominations may be made from the floor with consent from the nominee.

Section 4: Officers and directors shall be elected by a majority vote of those present at the annual meeting.

Section 5: Vacancies occurring on the Board of Directors shall be filled for the unexpired term thereof by a majority vote of the remaining members of the Board of Directors.

ARTICLE V - AMENDMENTS

Section 1: This Constitution and By-Laws may be amended by the majority of the members voting on such an amendment.

ARTICLE VI - FINANCES

Section 1: Moneys received from memberships, projects, gifts, and memorials shall be used to further the purposes of this organization.

Section 2: All funds of the organization shall be deposited from time to time to the credit of the organization in such banks as the Board of Directors may select.

Section 3: All expenditures from these funds shall be approved by the Board of Directors.

Section 4: The fiscal year shall be from January 1 through December 31 of each year.

Section 5: No part of the net earnings of the organization shall inure to the benefit of, or be distributable to, its members, trustees, officers, or other private persons, except that the organization shall be authorized and empowered to pay reasonable compensation for services rendered.

ARTICLE VII - DISSOLUTION

Upon dissolution of the organization the Board of Directors, after paying or making provisions for the payment of all of the liabilities and obligations of the organization, shall transfer or convey all remaining assets to the Happy Hollow Public Library.

If the Happy Hollow Public Library is no longer in existence or is unable or unwilling to receive the assets, the remaining assets shall be distributed to an organization which at the time qualifies as an exempt organization under Section 501 (c) (3) of the Internal Revenue Code, or to a governmental unit for a public purpose.

SAMPLE BY-LAWS

ARTICLE 1 - MEETINGS

Section 1: The annual meeting shall be held in December. Members shall be notified in writing at least two weeks prior to the date of the meeting.

Section 2: Meetings of the Board of Directors shall be held throughout the year on specific dates agreed on by the Directors.

Section 3: A simple majority of the Board of Directors shall constitute a quorum.

Section 4: The agency head or a delegated representative shall be present at all meetings.

Section 5: All meetings shall be open to the public.

ARTICLE II - DUTIES OF OFFICERS AND DIRECTORS

Section 1: The President shall:
(A) Preside at all meetings.
(B) With the consent of the Board of Directors, appoint all committee chairpersons and coordinate their activities.

(C) Represent the Friends before any group requesting presence of the Friends, or delegate a representative.

(D) Be an ex-officio member of all committees except the nominating committee.

(E) Prepare a brief annual report to include information on the activities of the past year and an announcement of the date of the annual meeting in October.

(F) Appoint with consent of the Board of Directors a representative and an alternate to the Friends Council to serve for one year.

Section 2: The Vice President shall:

(A) Preside at meetings and perform the duties of the President in the absence of the President.

Section 3: The Secretary shall:

(A) Keep the minutes of all Board and Annual meetings and distribute them to all Board members, the community librarian, and the Executive Board of the Friends Council.

(B) Conduct all correspondence as directed by the President.

(C) Perform such other duties as are customary of the office of Secretary

Section 4: The Treasurer shall:

(A) Be the chief financial officer of the organization.

(B) Make regular financial reports to the Board of Directors.

(C) Keep an account of all money received by the organization and deposit the same in the bank designated by the Board.

(D) Pay all bills as approved by the Board of Directors.

(E) Act as membership chairman, collect all dues, maintain a current list of paid members, and regularly inform the Board of the status of the membership.

(F) Perform such other duties as the Board of Directors may from time to time prescribe.

ARTICLE III - DUTIES OF STANDING COMMITTEES

Section 1: The Program Chairperson shall:

(A) Cooperate with the librarian in the selection and presentation of informational, educational, recreational programs and events according to the guidelines set forth in the Happy Hollow Public Library Programming Policy. Approval of sponsorship and/or events shall be granted by a majority vote of the Board of Directors.

(B) Act as hospitality chairperson in coordinating all social arrangements, welcoming speakers and guests, and performing other duties as directed by the President.

Section 2: The Telephone Chairperson shall:

(A) Notify and/or remind members of meetings, call for volunteers from the membership when needed for special projects, and aid the Treasurer in organizing membership drives.

Section 3: The Special Projects Chairperson shall:

(A) Initiate special community-oriented projects with the approval of the Board.

(B) Organize committees to carry out projects.

ARTICLE IV - DUES STRUCTURE

Section 1: Dues shall be payable annually.

Section 2: Dues shall be:

> Individual, $5.00
> Junior Friends, $1.00
> Family, $7.50
> Sustaining, $25
> Business and Organization, $50
> Life Membership, $100.00

Friends of the Library can be very helpful to a library director and the library board—especially when each has a clear understanding of their respective roles.

FOUNDATIONS

The purpose of a library foundation is to receive money, particularly large sums, charitable trusts, and bequests. The money is invested, and the proceeds go to the library each year. A foundation usually does not have a large membership, but everyone on the board should be committed to fundraising to the point of making regular contributions themselves.

Friends of the library and the library foundation come into conflict when roles overlap or are not understood. Friends earn money and spend it as the need arises. The foundation receives donations and invests them to proved a stable future for the library. Friends do visible things with their money. The foundation normally turns the proceeds of investments over to the library, for library purposes. Together they can cooperate to help the library achieve its short-term and long-term goals.

If you are serious about organizing a foundation to support your library, get a copy of *First Steps in Starting a Foundation* by John Edie.

IRS 501 (C) (3) DESIGNATION.

One essential element of a foundation is the IRS 501 (c) (3) designation. Start by contacting your regional office of the Internal Revenue Service. Ask them for Application for Recognition of Exemption under Section 501 (c) (3) of the Internal Revenue Code. Your foundation must have been in operation for 15 months before you can have this designation. Don't be intimidated by the process of filling out the forms. Just take everything one step at a time. Ask for help if you need it. Some corporate donors absolutely require a copy of the letter designating your foundation as as 501 (c) (3) agency.

You will want the advice of a lawyer when you organize a foundation. You may even want one to help you draft the by-laws. Organization of a foundation follows much the same pattern as a Friends group, except that you will not have as many members.

Here is a sample constitution and by-laws document.

SAMPLE BYLAWS

ARTICLE I — NAME AND LOCATION

Section 1. The name of the corporation is the Singing Rock Public Library Foundation.

Section 2. General Office. The general and principal office of the Foundation in this state shall be located at the Singing Rock Public Library, 1409 Williams, Singing Rock, KS 66679.

Section 3. Other Offices. In addition to its principal office in this state, the Foundation may maintain offices at any other place or places designated by the Board of Trustees within the State of Kansas.

Section 4. Corporate Seal. The Foundation may have a seal upon which shall be inscribed its name and the words "Corporate Seal".

Section 5. Resident Agent. The name and address of the resident agent of the Foundation is _____, 1409 Williams, Singing Rock, KS 66679.

ARTICLE II — PURPOSE

Section 1. Basic Purpose. The Foundation shall have as its basic purpose the promotion of the continued growth and improvement of the welfare, general public relations and for increasing the size and number of the holdings of library materials of the Singing Rock Public Library.

Section 2. Ancillary Purposes. The Foundation shall, in pursuit of its basic purpose, engage in the following pursuits:

(a) To establish and maintain an endowment fund for the benefit of the Singing Rock Public Library.

(b) To encourage individuals and organizations to make financial contributions to support the Singing Rock Public Library, and to accept, acknowledge and approve each and every gift either in money or material regardless of size or form.

(c) To establish, promote, maintain, endow and render aid and assistance, financial or otherwise, to the Singing Rock Public Library.

(d) To establish certain memorials in cooperation with the donors.

(e) To purchase, for the Singing Rock Public Library, library materials, or to make funds available for such purposes.

(f) To accept only such gifts of property or material as the donor may consent to the Board of Trustees converting into money.

(g) To establish two types of funds. The first and primary fund shall be the endowment fund or funds, which shall be invested for the highest possible income of good security, the income of which only shall be transferred to the second fund. The second fund shall be the working fund from which all purchases and expenses shall be paid. It shall receive the earnings of the endowment funds and all such incidental gifts and income that may be found to be too small to constitute the formation of an endowment fund and whose donors have expressed no desires as to the disposition of such funds.

(h) In the event of dissolution, to make contributions to organizations that qualify as exempt charitable, educational, or scientific organizations under Section 501 (c) (3) of the I.R.C. of 1954 (or the corresponding provision of any future U. S. Internal Revenue law).

ARTICLE III — TRUSTEES

Section 1. The business and property of the Foundation shall be managed by the Board of Trustees as stated in the Articles of Incorporation. The Board of Trustees shall be composed of at least seven (7) individuals, elected by the Board of Directors of the Singing Rock Public Library at the annual meeting of said board. Trustees' terms shall ordinarily be for three (3) years. The terms of the Trustees shall be staggered so that at least two Trustees are elected at each annual meeting. The number of terms that a Trustee may serve is unlimited.

Section 2. Trustees shall be residents of the State of Kansas. Trustees shall have served or be serving on the Board of Trustees of the Singing Rock Public Library.

Section 3. An annual meeting of the Board of Trustees shall be held each year upon the call of the chairman.

Section 4. A special meeting of the Board of Trustees may be called at any time or place by the chairman or vice-chairman, or in their absence or inability to act, the same may be called by any two members of the Board. By unanimous consent of the Trustees, regular or special meetings of the Board of Trustees may be held without notice of any time or place.

Section 5. Notice of all regular and special meetings shall be mailed to each Trustee by the Secretary at least two days previous to the time fixed for such meeting. All notices of special meeting shall state the purpose thereof and the time and place where the meeting is to be held.

Section 6. A quorum for the transaction of business at any meeting of the Board of Trustees shall consist of the majority of the members of the Board; but the Trustees, although less than a quorum, shall have the power to adjourn the meeting from day to day or to some future date.

Section 7. Whenever a vacancy shall occur in the Board of Trustees by death, resignation or otherwise, the same shall be filled without undue delay by a majority vote of the Board of Trustees of the Singing Rock Public Library.

Section 8. Any Trustee may be removed, with or without cause, by the vote of two-thirds (2/3) of the members of the Board of Trustees of the Singing Rock Public Library at any special meeting called for the purpose, at which meeting any vacancy caused by such removal may be filled.

ARTICLE IV — OFFICERS

Section 1. The officers of the Foundation shall consist of a chairman, a vice-chairman, a secretary and a treasurer, and such other officers as shall, from time to time, be provided by the Board of Trustees. The office of secretary and treasurer may be held by the same person.

The officers shall be chosen from among the Trustees. All officers shall be chosen by the Board of Trustees of the Foundation at the annual meeting of such Board, or at such other meeting of said Board as may be called for that purpose. The chairman and vice-chairman shall hold office until the next annual meeting of the Board of Trustees and until their respective successors are elected and qualified. The chairman and vice-chairman may serve unlimited consecutive terms. All other officers of the Foundation shall hold office at the pleasure of the Board of Trustees.

Section 2. Chairman. The chairman shall preside at all meetings of the Board of Trustees and shall have general supervision of the affairs of the Foundation and shall see that all orders and resolutions of the Board are carried into effect.

Section 3. Vice-Chairman. In the absence, disability or under the direction of the chairman, the vice-chairman shall be vested with all the powers and perform all the duties of the chairman, and shall have such additional powers and perform such additional duties as shall be ordered by the Board of Trustees.

Section 4. Secretary. The secretary shall give or cause to be given all required notices of meetings of the Board of Trustees, except as otherwise provided in these Bylaws; shall record all proceedings at the meetings of the Board of Trustees in a book to be kept for that purpose; and shall perform such other duties as may be assigned to him by the chairman or Board of Trustees. The secretary shall have custody of the seal of the Foundation, if one is issued, and shall affix the same to all instruments when duly authorized to do so and attest to same, and do and perform such additional duties as may be ordered by the Board of Trustees.

Section 5. Treasurer. The treasurer shall have the custody of all moneys, valuable papers and documents of the Foundation, shall place the same for safekeeping in such depositories as may be designed by the Board of Trustees. The treasurer shall expend the funds of the Foundation as directed by the Board of Trustees, taking proper vouchers for such expenditures, shall keep or cause to be kept, a book or books setting forth a true record of the receipts, expenditures, assets, liabilities, losses and gains of the Foundation and shall, when and as required by the chairman of the Board of Trustees, render a statement of the financial condition of the Foundation and cause to be filed appropriate tax returns. As a requirement to serve as treasurer of the Foundation, the treasurer shall procure an appropriate bond in an amount to be determined by the Board of Trustees, from an insurer authorized to transact business in this state.

ARTICLE V — ADVISORY BOARD OF TRUSTEES

Section 1. Advisory Board: There shall be a committee known as the Advisory Board of Trustees consisting of not less than one (1) nor more than nine (9) persons of varied ages and abilities, appointed by the Board of Trustees for terms of one (1) year or until successors are chosen.

Section 2. The Board of Trustees shall select individuals interested in the promotion and improvement of the Singing Rock Public Library as Advisory Trustees.

Section 3. Said Advisory Board of Trustees shall meet at least annually on the call and proper notice of the chairman of such Advisory Board of Trustees.

Section 4. The purpose of the Advisory Board of Trustees shall be to give to the Board of Trustees reports and suggestions as to the continued and future efforts of said Foundation.

Section 5. The Board of Trustees shall appoint a chairman of the Advisory Board of Trustees. The Advisory Board of Trustees shall select a vice-chairman and secretary from its members.

ARTICLE VI

Section 1. These Bylaws may be amended upon a vote of the majority of a quorum of the Trustees of the Singing Rock Public Library present at any annual meeting of such Board, or at any special meeting thereof, when proper notice of such proposed amendment has been given.

SUMMARY

Every library can benefit from a Friends of the library group and a foundation. Start with a Friends group, if you have neither. As the need arises establish a foundation. Friends create better visibility for the library, and they give an opportunity for many people to become involved with the inner workings of the library. Their efforts as fundraisers will vary from community to community, but their presence tells townspeople the library is important to more people than just the board and the library staff.

15 CONSULTANTS

In days when pioneers were moving west, they would send scouts ahead of the main company to figure out the best route to follow. Usually mounted on fast horses, scouts looked for the most feasible places to cross rivers and good locations to camp. Sometimes they would climb high peaks so they could see far into the distance. Sometimes they stopped and talked with other travelers. They were always on the lookout for dangers. The job of the the scout was to get the wagon train to its destination with the least difficulty.

Every fundraising effort needs a scout. If you are that person, find a fast horse and saddle up. If not, find someone else to lead your project. You need someone who has experience with fundraising to help you through the mine field. Fundraising consultant Robert Hartsook says, "If you don't think you have the expertise within your organization, get some help." To some degree this book can be your scout, but you still need a knowledgeable person to help you make it all the way across the plains. Consider these possibilities:

A local full-time fundraiser for another organization: Most colleges have a development department. It may be called by a variety of names—foundation, scholarship fund, or development department. Their job is to raise money for the college—primarily for scholarships or building expansion. Sometimes they will be willing to meet with others and share their expertise—especially if they do not perceive your campaign as a threat to them. They realize that they cannot be the recipient of all local giving. They may even see your effort as an enhancement of their fundraising.

A volunteer head of the United Way: Often these people have abundant experience in the area of fundraising. If they are convinced of the value of your cause, they can be very helpful. Local people already know your turf. It may be easier for them to understand your needs and help you develop a strategy for your community.

Consultants from the state library or the system: If you belong to a system that provides consulting services, you may be able to get some good help from them. Your state library may also offer consulting assistance. Either way, these consultants have a responsibility to help all libraries in the area. Some consultants may lack specific fundraising skills, but they are usually competent in the areas of library development, community analysis, planning, leadership training and using volunteers. They can help you organize and get started. They will know your area better than someone from out of state.

As part of my job as the administrator for the Central Kansas

Library System, I have helped several libraries in Kansas organize their fundraising effort. I have helped write successful grants, develop charts of giving, write fundraising letters, train and motivate volunteers, and analyze community resources. I have taught planning skills, goal setting, group decision-making and fundraising—helping librarians and trustees to find ways to increase their revenue from all sources.

Commitment and follow-through are the big variables with anyone who works for an organization outside of your community. Though our consultants are as accessible as a toll-free call and we can usually attend a meeting when needed, it is impossible to devote full time and attention to the needs of a single library for more than a few hours at a time. Because of other pressing responsibilities, consultants not under contract to you may not be able to devote enough time or energy to your project. If they do a good job of training you and your fundraising group, you may not need additional help.

Professional fundraising consultants: Many librarians and board members are afraid hiring a professional fundraiser because they believe that the community will react negatively toward them and they don't want to jeopardize their fundraising effort. It is important that the librarian, the board, and the community understand that professional consultants do no soliciting.

The Beaver Dam Library in Wisconsin hired a professional fundraiser to do a feasibility study, write a campaign booklet, and find a volunteer chairman. In the leadership phase, they recruited 17 volunteers to solicit approximately 75 prospects. In the special phase, they recruited 70 volunteers to solicit approximately 250 prospects. They also did a phone-a-thon using volunteers and the city directory. An attempt was made to call everyone in the city. The public response to the professional fundraiser was excellent.

Eloise Hart of the Heart of America Fund Development Consultants, summarizes the advantages of using a professional fundraising consultant: "Most organizations lack the staff with time and expertise to organize and plan a major campaign. Consultants can obtain more accurate information from the community about the library. They have well-developed skills to train and motivate volunteers."

A professional consulting firm will send experts into your area to help you organize and execute a fundraising campaign. They will move you through every step of the process, and if you follow their guidance, you will raise money. Most work for a set fee. Those who are members of the National Society of Fundraising

Executives or the American Association of Fundraising Counsel subscribe to a code of fair practice that prohibits them from charging a percentage of the funds raised.

AAFRC FAIR PRACTICE CODE

Member firms of the American Association of Fundraising Counsel respect the American philanthropic tradition and the central role of men and women who founded our voluntary organizations, govern them, and are responsible for their financial support.

The member firms view the role of professional consultants as one of assisting and supporting the volunteers in their fundraising responsibilities and strengthening their capabilities as leaders and solicitors.

Purpose. The purpose of the Code is to set forth fundraising tenets which member firms are expected to follow.

Membership. Firms exclusively or primarily organized to provide fundraising counsel and direction are eligible for membership in the AAFRC. To qualify, firms must meet and maintain high standards of performance and demonstrate a record of success.

Services Provided. Member firms provide fundraising counsel, conduct feasibility and planning studies, and offer campaign management, public relations and other related services. Services are provided to 501(c) (3) organizations whose purpose and practices are deemed to be in the public interest. Member firms do not engage in methods that are misleading to the public or harmful to their clients; do not make exaggerated claims of past achievements; and do not guarantee results or promise to helps clients achieve unrealistic goals.

Payment of Services. Member firms believe it is in the best interest of clients that:

- Fees be mutually agreed upon in advance and that they be based on the level and extent of services provided, except that initial meetings with prospective clients are not usually construed as services for which payment is expected;
- Contracts providing for a contingent fee, commission or percentage of funds raised be avoided; and
- The services of professional solicitors who receive a contingent fee, commission or percentage of funds raised, be avoided.

Further:

- Member firms also believe it is in the best interest of clients that solicitation of gifts should generally be undertaken by volunteers.
- Member firms should not profit directly or indirectly from materials provided by others but billed through the member firms.
- No payment should be made to an officer, director, trustee, employee or advisor of a nonprofit organization as compensation for influencing the selection of fundraising counsel.
- Any potential conflict of interest should be disclosed to clients and prospective clients.

This code of conduct has set the standard for all professional fundraising consultants. Some reputable professional consultants are not members of the Association, but they subscribe to the Code of Fair Practice anyway. Ask them if they embrace this code, and get it in writing before signing a contract.

A detailed agreement outlines their services and the fee for each component. Costs vary, but usually run between six and 15 percent of the total amount raised. Some professional fundraisers guarantee that their fees will not exceed ten percent of the money you raise. If you want to raise $500,000, count on spending between $30,000 and $50,000. The higher the goal, the lower the percentage.

Most professional fundraisers will do a feasibility study first. Dick Hedberg of Dick Hedberg and Associates absolutely requires a feasibility study before entering into a contract to assist with a fundraising effort. From experience, they know within a few thousand dollars how much money can be raised. If they have doubts about the success of a fundraising effort, they discuss their reservations with the client before proceeding. They may suggest waiting a few months or a year. They may have some suggestions for improved relations with the community or ways to rebuild credibility. When the feasibility study gives you a green light, the professional will draw up a contract offering the following components:

- Help find the volunteer leader
- Organize the campaign
- Train the volunteers

PROFESSIONAL FUNDRAISER READINESS QUIZ

1. Do we want to raise less than $250,000?

2. Do we have a clear vision of what we want to do and how we want to do it?

3. Do members of our organization have the skills to assess the giving potential for our project in our community?

4. Do we know who will lead us and are we confident that he or she can manage the campaign?

5. Can we train our volunteers to be highly effective solicitors?

6. Can we count on every member of the board to be committed to the project?

7. Can we recruit people to help us sell our vision to others in a way that will raise money?

8. Do we have the skills and resources within our organization to develop quality written materials to support our project?

9. Can we write and produce a persuasive, polished case statement?

- Set the campaign calendar
- Provide public relations services.

You will have to learn what services the fundraiser has to offer and pick from those you feel meet your needs. Talk to other people who have used the fundraising firm you are considering. Learn from their experiences, but remember that every community is different and you are the expert in yours. Whether you hire a professional or not is up to you.

Take this quiz to see if you really want to explore the possibility of hiring a professional fundraiser. If you answered "yes" to all of these questions, you may not need a professional fundraiser. The first question is critical. Raising less than $250,000 can probably be done on your own. That is not to say that you can't benefit from the assistance of a professional. Tom Vance, of Kenneth M. Vance Fundraising Consultants of LeMars, Iowa, feels that the return on the investment below this amount is questionable.

He says: "Raising major dollar support is much like restoring an irreplaceable book: it involves meticulous planning and perseverance. The process of formulating needs, building an effective appeal, and raising major funding requires leadership exhibiting three traits:

"*Desire to learn*—taking in; soaking up; becoming full of knowledge pertaining to your institution: where you've been; where you're going, and how you're going to get there.

"*Providing challenge and vision*—leading; inspiring others to seek and achieve.

"*Discipline*—planning; executing; persevering through to the completion of the goal."

Whether you hire a professional or seek the advice of someone else, you should expect your consultant to:

- Do a feasibility study
- Review and refine your library's mission statement
- Interview community leaders
- Help select campaign leaders
- Assist in setting a realistic goal for project
- Help write and prepare case statement
- Formulate gift brackets to reach the goal
- Train leaders to recruit volunteers
- Train volunteer solicitors
- Help get the campaign started
- Keep the campaign moving
- Manage the campaign office

- Formulate the total campaign calendar
- Provide guidance for large gift cultivation
- Write special proposals
- Prepare public relations materials
- Develop follow-up procedures.

CONDUCTING A FEASIBILITY STUDY

You will want to do a feasibility study before contracting with a professional fundraiser for a full blown campaign. A reputable fundraiser will want to do this as a first step. Vance Associates says: "The pre-campaign study is the prelude to the actual campaign. It forms the foundation and direction for all planning. It answers the following questions:

- How much money can be raised?
- Where are the funds coming from?
- Who will be the most effective chairperson?
- What is the best timetable?

Most of all—it begins the process of building ownership in the campaign."

The time requirements for an effective pre-campaign study will vary depending on the geographical location of the institution's constituency and the number of interviews conducted. The professionals begin with a short list of community leaders as a starting point. The list is generated from a meeting of community leaders who have an interest in the organization. As they interview members of this group, they ask for the names of community leaders. They get a sense of the community and its attitudes about the organization. They also gain an awareness of where the big money is. All the time they are looking for the person perceived by the community to be the best leader of the fundraising campaign. This is one of the strongest advantages of using a professional fundraiser. The library board may have hand-picked someone for the task, yet the community may not perceive that person to be the most effective one for the job. An outsider, helping to select the leader for the campaign, can add credibility to the effort and help overcome the possibility of cronyism.

Dick Hedberg likes to interview at least 30 people. First of all, he asks the individuals how they feel about the library. Is it meeting their needs? Could it do a better job? If so, how? He takes two documents with him—a list of library needs and their estimated costs and a scale of giving. After reviewing the list of needs with the person he is interviewing, he explains that in order for the library to

PRELIMINARY QUESTIONS

Here are some of the questions Vance Associates ask selected community leaders in the feasibility study:

- How do you perceive the library and its services?

- How is the library perceived by others?

- To what extent do you know about the library's plans?

- Do you consider them feasible?

- What levels of financial support might you consider?

- When is the best time to mount an effort?

- Who is the strongest leader?

meet its needs, it has to raise so much money. Then he shows them the scale of giving and asks how many gifts of a certain size they think can be raised in the community. Sometimes, without asking, they volunteer to make the lead gift. What a nice surprise!

Patricia Pawl, director of Wisconsin's Beaver Dam Public Library, says that her library used a professional fundraiser to help raise $425,000 in her community of 15,000 people. Their feasibility study, which was critical to the success of the campaign, cost $5,000. The range is from $5,000 to $15,000. It is better to spend $5,000 on a study that tells you to shape up your performance and your image in the community before mounting a major campaign than to fail in the attempt. Tom Vance says, "If you do start and the effort fails, it is difficult to go back and pick up the pieces."

Dick Hedberg says, "A feasibility study does the following:

- It tells you how much you can raise.
- It tells you how long it will take.
- It gives you a budget for the campaign.
- It lets you know if you have the volunteers to do the job.
- It pre-sells the need to prospective donors without asking them for money."

Part of the feasibility study is selecting the right leadership. Some campaigns flounder because of the wrong leadership. Notice I said the wrong leadership, not poor leadership nor the lack of leadership. Sometimes community pacesetters are good leaders but they just aren't right to lead a major fundraising campaign for the library. When a professional fundraiser asks 30 people in a community who would be the preeminent leader for a library fundraising campaign, he will hear three or four names mentioned more often than the rest. The most effective leader will usually be among those interviewed.

REFINING THE MISSION STATEMENT

A consultant who has interviewed 25 people in the community will be able to offer an outsider's view of how the public sees the mission of the library. Too often, the librarian and board members see the mission of the library from an insider's perspective rather than the user's view. If the library's mission statement lacks vision, the consultant will discover the weakness and help strengthen it by offering the view of the people. You have to know where you are headed before you can lead the way for others.

SETTING A GOAL

Vance Associates use a pre-campaign questionnaire with library board members to help clarify their thinking. Here are the questions they ask:

1. Does the library board presently have a mission statement?
2. What are some past notable achievements of the library?
3. What are the library's physical plant needs?
4. What are the library's maintenance needs?
5. What are the library's endowment needs?
6. What are the library's staffing needs?
7. What are the library's program and service needs?
8. Are the architect's cost estimates complete?
9. Has a five- to ten-year financial forecast been completed, taking into account costs generated by contemplated goals?
10. Are operating income projections realistic?
11. What are the board's capabilities?
12. Are they willing to work for the effort?
13. What level of goodwill for the library presently exists within the community?
14. What is the volunteer base?
15. What have been the results of past efforts?
16. What is the time table for raising funds?

Completing a project outline form further clarifies the board's thinking.

Assigning a dollar figure to each fiscal question is the basis for setting the fundraising goal. It is extremely important not to overlook any cost regardless of how obscure it is or how insignificant it may seem. Architectural fees often run more than ten percent of the cost of the building, yet they are often overlooked in the early planning stages. Duplicating the plans and specification are not usually included as part of the architect's fee. They can run several hundred dollars. Those who have been through the process several times can guide you through the swamp and around the quicksand as you figure out what it will take to complete your project.

PREPARING THE CASE STATEMENT

If this is the first time you are writing a case statement, the help of a professional may be worth every cent. Patricia Pawl paid $2,000 to have someone write the case statement for the Beaver Dam Public

Library's campaign and then spent another $1,000 to have it printed. She considered the effort essential to the campaign. This is a critical document. Next to the people who carry it to potential donors, it's the most visible representation of your library. It has to look good. Your case statement can make a difference in the size and number of gifts.

PREPARING PUBLIC RELATIONS MATERIALS

You will need news releases, brochures, and other materials to give to donors. The best is not too good to represent your library. Anyone can write a news release. Writing one that will be used by the newspaper the way you write it is a special skill. Question: If you already write a lot for your library, why turn it over to the professionals? Answer: They may be able to give your project a new slant you haven't thought of.

My experience with public relations tells me that cheap can be very expensive when you are trying to influence those with power and money. People are not impressed by your poverty. Your publicity pieces have to look good—printed on a good grade of paper.

FORMULATING THE GIFT BRACKETS

Early on in the process, the consultant will sit down with your group and complete this critical document. He or she will use it, without names, as part of the feasibility study. Eventually you will have to have a name on every blank (three names for every gift you expect) and solicit them before you publicly announce the campaign. See the Chart of Giving in Chapter 7.

The feasibility study will yield valuable information to help develop your chart of giving. If your fundraiser asks 25 people how many $10,000, $5,000 and $1,000 gifts can be expected in your community, the answers will cluster on a norm and provide a good target for your gift brackets. It will also help you predict how much money you can raise.

CULTIVATING LARGE GIFTS

Forty percent of your money will come from 18 to 20 donors. Big donors take special cultivation. If a professional fundraiser can help you turn a $25,000 donation into a $50,000, her fee will have been paid for in one gift. When your largest category of giving is $1,000, you may have cheated yourself out of $49,000 by not doing your homework or targeting a gift more suited to the donor's potential. It is difficult to go back to someone who has given a moderate amount and ask them to give more. Some professionals will accompany a volunteer to solicit a big gift.

Project Outline Form

Name of library:_____

Present facility built:_____

Project planning started:_____

Deficiencies in present facility:_____

_____

_____

_____

_____

Building plans:_____

Architect:_____

Exterior rendition available:_____

Floor plan available:_____

Completion date goal:_____

Estimated total project cost:_____

    Building:_____

    Furnishings:_____

    Equipment:_____

    Endowment:_____

Projected annual maintenance cost:_____

    Paid for by:_____

Sources of project funding (Planning estimates)

Private funding:_____

City:_____

Future bonding:_____

County:_____

Grants:_____

Other:_____

Library usage

Total circulation for most recent year:_____

Previous year:_____

Five year trend: Up_____Down_____Even_____

Areas of greatest growth:_____

Three strengths of present program:

_____

_____

_____

_____

_____

_____

Three weaknesses:

_____

_____

_____

_____

_____

_____

What existing programs will be strengthened or new programs established if project is completed:

_____

_____

_____

_____

_____

_____

Source: Vance Associates, LeMars, IA.

TRAINING VOLUNTEERS

It is easier to recruit volunteers than to train them to be effective solicitors. It may be a good idea to rely on someone who has done it several times before. One librarian said that her fundraising consultant did three different training sessions—one for the big gifts committee, one for the medium gifts committee, and one for the telephone soliciting group. Each training session was specifically tailored to the needs of the volunteers and their targeted donors.

FORMULATING THE CAMPAIGN CALENDAR

Most campaigns drag on too long. People get discouraged, not because they have failed, but because they have put off the task of asking for money. Fearing failure, volunteers lose their initial enthusiasm and what seemed exciting at first has now become drudgery. Vance Associates likes to set a 12-week maximum for wrapping up; the whole fund drive is wrapped up, from initial contacts to follow-up. That doesn't mean that all of the money is in, because some gifts are in the form of pledges. Collecting them may extend for up to five years. The key is setting a realistic but tight schedule, generating enthusiasm among the volunteers, training them, and then letting them go out to get the money. A member of the Vance team keeps the effort moving by staying with the project from beginning to end.

Most volunteer fundraisers have other responsibilities. They have jobs to do, social activities, and families who need them. They usually can't give full time to a major fundraising project. Since a professional is being paid to oversee the campaign, it becomes his job to keep people on schedule, to motivate and support them.

STARTING THE CAMPAIGN

"Overcoming inertia is the most difficult part of any campaign," says Tom Vance. Someone has to say, "Ready, set, go!" If you do it too soon or too late, you lose the continuity of a well-scheduled effort. You have to get off to a good start and keep moving until the goal is reached. You don't want your team to run out of gas before the end of the race. Neither do you want to get them all enthused and then make them wait two weeks for printed materials.

MANAGING THE CAMPAIGN OFFICE

Once volunteers are trained and have started bringing in money and pledges, someone has to be in the office to receive the gifts and provide backup for special situations. One library hired a part-time secretary to handle the extra paperwork generated by the campaign. The professional fundraiser provided technical assistance on other matters. Most librarians are already burdened down with more than they can handle. Running a major fundraising campaign is like taking on another full-time job. Unless you have some very dedicated volunteers with lots of time to give away, you may want to hire someone to run the campaign office and handle the extra paper work.

FOLLOW-UP PROCEDURES

After the campaign is completed, your money will still be coming in. Pledges will have to be collected. A professional can help you develop the forms you need to follow through on pledges and incoming donations. Regular well-worded form letters and re-minders will keep the money coming in until it has all been collected. If you raise $400,000 in cash and pledges, you won't have $400,000 until the last pledge is paid.

WORKING WITH THE PROFESSIONAL

Most professional fundraisers are skilled leaders and trainers. They earn their money by organizing the campaign and helping the volunteers execute the plan. Tom Vance says, "It is easy to raise the first 25 percent of a fundraising campaign. Anyone can do that. The professionals help you get the last 75 percent."

One librarian said, "I don't want people to think they can hire a professional fundraiser and not do any work. It takes a lot of work to raise a lot of money." She suggests that the key to a capital fund drive is the volunteer chair. "We had a volunteer chairman who was liked by everyone in the community. He followed through on all tasks promptly. He was able to recruit the dozens and dozens of volunteers needed to make a fund drive work," she said. The professional fundraiser provides the forms and a time frame to keep the fund drive on track. There is a big misunderstanding among many people that the professional fundraiser relieves the trustees or volunteers of work. The professional fundraiser does not solicit or do their work.

DONOR CULTIVATION

If your pre-campaign assessment tells you and your professional fundraiser that you have some work to do before mounting a major campaign, you may want to engage in a donor cultivation program. Some professionals offer this as one of their services. The purpose of this program is to prepare your organization and community for a major capital or endowment effort. The program can last from six months to two years.

Here is how it works:

CULTIVATE YOUR COMMUNITY

The professionals provide direction to cultivate your community in anticipation of a major campaign. They give guidance in considering and building a foundation board, steering committee, and with other methods of getting the right people and resources involved in your project.

DEVELOP YOUR APPEAL

They offer input into the decision-making process as you plan for your future project. They look at your proposed project and financial need and help you develop an effective appeal for your community.

PRESS RELEASES

Every two weeks they provide you with press releases for the media in your community. These releases are uniquely suited for your organization and community with one goal in mind—to build the strongest case for future success.

SPECIAL DONORS

The professionals will create and produce individualized quarterly mailings. These communications are designed to cultivate individuals with the potential to provide major support to your future campaign.

MEETINGS WITH THE BOARD

They will meet with your board every six months to help maintain interest and provide assistance in the planning process.

HIRING A FUNDRAISING CONSULTANT

When we hire someone, we usually review our job requirements and look for the person who best matches those requirements. The problem with hiring a fundraising consultant is that you probably have never done it before and you don't know where to start. You don't know enough about the job requirements of fundraising to make a good decision. It is unlikely that you can pick up your telephone directory and find a professional fundraiser listed in the

Selecting a Consultant

QUESTIONS TO ASK

Does the fundraising consultant:

1. Initiate pro-active responses to change?

2. Focus on the goals of your library?

3. Try to understand your needs before trying to impress you with his skill?

4. Seek to organize and clarify needs?

5. Seek for a variety of solutions?

6. Initiate action by suggesting alternative solutions?

7. Consider the need in the context of the community?

8. Build on strengths rather than assess blame for a bad situation?

9. Encourage and support local efforts?

10. Challenge accepted thinking in a constructive way?

11. Possess relevant people skills?

yellow pages, though that is a good place to start. The National Association of Fundraising Counsel, Inc., 25 West 43rd Street, New York, NY 10036, will send you a list of their member firms. The National Society of Fundraising Executives, 1101 King Street, Suite 3000, Alexandria, VA 22314, will also send you a list of their members, who are professional fundraising consultants.

Selecting fundraising counsel is like getting married. You need to get acquainted. Ask a lot of questions and test your own feelings. How do you feel when you are around the person? Do you feel comfortable? Would you like to be around him or her more?

Dick Hedberg says, "Most important of all is the chemistry of the people. Is the consultant going to represent you in the community the way you want him to and how will he work with the head of your organization?"

Here is a list of questions to ask yourself after you become acquainted with the consultant. They will help you clarify your feelings.

If you and your board feel good about the prospective consultant, after having asked these questions and after having spent some time with him or her, go ahead with the contract. You have probably made a good choice. On the other hand if you have what I call "fuzzy" feelings, wait a while. If these feelings stay with you, find another prospect.

SUMMARY

The decision to hire a professional fundraising consultant depends on how much money you want to raise. If you want to raise $250,000 or more, give it serious consideration. Don't hire a professional to make up for a lack of community support or a lack of willing volunteers. Remember: a professional won't do the work for you. He or she will just help you organize and teach you how to be more effective.

CONCLUSION

Steven Covey in his audiocassette seminar, *Seven Basic Habits of Highly Effective People,* suggests new ways a looking at the world. I trust that *Fundraising for the Small Public Library* has given you a more hopeful vision of your world. If you want to be successful as a library fundraiser, try Dr. Covey's Seven Basic Habits. Here they are:

Be proactive. Do something. Act rather than being acted upon.

Begin with the end in mind. Set goals. Work to achieve them.

Put first things first. It is more important to do the right things than to do things right.

Think win/win. Work for ways to help others win while accomplishing your own goals.

Seek first to understand (then to be understood). Learn to listen and understand the other's point of view.

Synergize. Work to make the whole more than the sum of its parts.

Sharpen the saw. Take time to develop the physical, emotional/social, spiritual and mental aspects of your life.

When you think about it, these seven habits are at the root of every good fundraising effort. I encourage you to secure the audiocassette series (or the book by the same title) and set a new course for your professional life and your library.

Go back to the Action Plan in the introduction and write down two or three ideas that impressed you as "do-able" in your library. Select the one that has the best chance for success. It might be to accelerate memorial giving. You can do it without involving too many other people and it will create new visibility for your library. You could complete the Building Needs Analysis Worksheet in Chapter 4 and share your findings with the board. It will make them aware of the need. Don't be ashamed to get some help if you need it. *Fundraising for the Small Public Library* was written as a how-to-do-it manual for librarians. It is an overview of the business of fundraising. Buy or borrow several of the books listed in the bibliography.

A young man, fresh out of college and armed with a degree in agriculture, was hired by a crop consulting firm to call on farmers and sell the services of his company. He went up to a farmer and said, "If you will sign up with my company, we will tell you when to plant, when to cultivate and when to irrigate. We can help you double your wheat crop and grow more corn at less cost than ever before. I will test your soil, tell you what fertilizer to use, and when to do it."

The old farmer thought a minute, then looked the agent right in the eye and said, "Sonny, we already don't do half as good as we know how."

The problem with so many library fundraisers is they don't put into practice what they already know how to do.

The fundraising ideas in this book are plentiful enough to keep the average librarian busy for years. I hope you found one or two that you can put to work for your library right away.

You can make a difference.

Do something!

BIBLIOGRAPHY

CAPITAL CAMPAIGNS

Ashton, Debra. *The Complete Guide to Planned Giving: Everything You Need to Know to Compete Successfully for Major Gifts.* Cambridge, Massachusetts: JLA Publications, 1988.

Hall, Frank. *Annual Giving Strategies.* Arcadia, California: Non-Profit Network. (Video)

Quigg, H. Gerald, ed. *The Successful Capital Campaign: from Planning to Victory Celebration.* Washington, D.C.: C.A.S.E, 1986.

DIRECT MAIL

Groman, John. *Direct Mail that Works!* Arcadia, California: Non-Profit Network. (Video)

Kuniholm, Roland. *Maximum Gifts by Return Mail.* Ambler, Pennsylvania: Fundraising Institute, 1989.

FRIENDS AND FOUNDATIONS

Ashfield, Jean A. *Friends of the Library Handbook.* Somersworth, New Hampshire: Friends of New Hampshire Libraries, 1980.

Dolnick, Sandy, ed. *Friends of Libraries Sourcebook.* Chicago: American Library Association, 1988.

Edie, John A. *First Steps in Starting a Foundation.* Washington, D.C.: Council on Foundations, 1987.

Wilson, Marlene. *The Effective Management of Volunteer Programs.* Boulder, Colorado: Volunteer Management Associates, 1976.

FUNDRAISING—GENERAL

Ardman, Perri and Harvey. *Woman's Day Book of Fundraising.* New York: St. Martin's Press, 1980.

Baker & Taylor Company. *Winning the Money Game.* New York: Baker and Taylor, 1979.

Broce, Thomas E. *Fundraising: The Guide to Raising Money from Private Sources.* 2nd ed. Norman, Oklahoma: University of Oklahoma Press, 1986.

Conrad, Daniel Lynn. *Successful Fundraising Techniques.* San Francisco: The Public Management Institute, 1977.

Ecton, Virgil. *Successful Special Events.* Arcadia, California: Non-Profit Network. (Video)

Flanagan, Joan, *The Grass Roots Fundraising Book*. Chicago, Illinois: Contemporary Books, 1982.

Plessner, Gerald M. *Fundraising Yesterday, Today and Tomorrow*. Arcadia, California: Non-Profit Network. (Video)

Schneiter, Paul H. *The Art of Asking: How to Solicit Philanthropic Gifts*. 2nd ed. Ambler, Pennsylvania: The Fundraising Institute, 1985.

Schneiter, Paul H. *The Thirteen Most Common Fundraising Mistakes and How to Avoid Them*. Washington, D.C.: The Taft Corporation, 1982.

Seymour, Harold J. *Designs for Fundraising*. 2nd ed. Ambler, Pennsylvania: The Fundraising Institute, 1988.

GRANTS

Bader, Barbara C. and Carr, Steven. *Get That Grant: Grantwriting from Conception to Completion*. Bozeman, Montana: Community Systems, 1987.

Bauer, David G. *The "How to" Grants Manual: Successful Grantseeking Techniques for Obtaining Public and Private Grants*. New York: Macmillan, 1988.

Bell, Dr. Norman T. and Dr. Frank Jackson. *Radio Shack's Proposal Writing Guide*. Tandy Corporation, 1981.

Boss, Richard W. *Grant Money and How to Get It*. New York, London: R. R. Bowker, 1980.

Conrad, Daniel Lynn. *The Quick Proposal Workbook: How to Produce Better Grant Proposals in 25-50% Less Time*. San Francisco: Public Management Institute, 1980.

Executive Office of the President, Office of Management and Budget. *1989 Catalog of Federal Domestic Assistance*. Washington, D.C.: U.S. General Services Administration, 1989.

Foundation Center, *Grants for Libraries and Information Services*. New York: The Foundation Center, 1989.

Hall, Mary. *Getting Funded: A Complete Guide to Proposal Writing*. 3rd ed. Portland: Continuing Education Publications, Portland State University, 1988.

Hillman, Howard and Karin Abarbanel. *The Art of Winning Foundation Grants*. New York: Vanguard Press, 1975.

Jankowski, Katherine, ed. *Corporate Giving Yellow Pages: the Complete Guide to Contact Persons*. 5th ed. Washington, D.C.: The Taft Group, 1988.

Lord, Benjamin W., ed. *America's Hidden Philanthropic Wealth*. 2nd ed. Washington, D.C.: The Taft Group, 1988.

Olson, Stan, ed. *The Foundation Directory*. 12th ed. New York: The Foundation Center, 1989.

Read, Patricia. *Foundation Fundamentals: A Guide for Grant Seekers,* 3rd ed. New York, The Foundation Center, 1986.

Sternberg, Sam. *National Directory of Corporate Charity*. San Francisco: Regional Young Adult Project, 1984.

The Taft Group. *Fund Raiser's Guide to Capital Grants*. 1st ed. Washington, D.C.: The Taft Group, 1988.

White, Virginia. *Grant Proposals That Succeeded*. New York: Plenum Press, 1983.

PLANNING

Childers, Thomas and Nancy Van House. *Public Library Effectiveness Study*. Philadelphia: Drexel University, 1989.

Curzon, Susan C. *Managing Change: A How-To-Do-It Manual for Planning, Implementing and Evaluating Change in Libraries*. New York, London: Neal-Schuman Publishers, 1989.

McClure, Charles R.; Amy Owen; Douglas L. Zweizig; Mary Jo Lynch; and, Nancy A. Van House. *Planning and Role Setting for Public Libraries*. Chicago, London: American Library Association, 1987.

Van House, Nancy A; Mary Jo Lynch; Charles R. McClure; Douglas L. Zweizig; and, Eleanor Jo Rodger. *Output Measures for Public Libraries*. 2nd ed. Chicago, London: American Library Association, 1987.

SMALL LIBRARIES

Bonnell, Pamela G. *Fundraising for the Small Library,* (Small libraries publication; Pamphlet # 8) Chicago: American Library Association, 1983.

Gervasi, Anne and Betty Kay Seibt. *Handbook for Small, Rural, and Emerging Public Libraries*. Phoenix, New York: Oryx Press, 1988.

Kadanoff, Diane Gordon. "Small Libraries—No Small Job!" *Library Journal*, March 1, 1986, 72-73.

Sheridan, Philip G. *Fundraising for the Small Organization*. New York: M. Evans and Company, 1968.

Swan, James. "Fundraising for the Small Public Library," *Wilson Library Bulletin*, April 1989, 46-48.

Swan, James. "New Visibility for the Small Public Library," *Wilson Library Bulletin*, January 1977, 424-27.

TRUSTEES

Lynch, Timothy P. "A Preliminary Survey of Library Board Trustees from Four Libraries in Pennsylvania," *Rural Libraries*, (Vol. VII, no. 11) 1987, 61-97.

O'Connell, Brian. *The Board Member's Book*. New York: The Foundation Center, 1985.

Richards, Audrey, series ed. *Board Member Trustee Handbook*. San Francisco: Public Management Institute, 1980.

Swan, James. "Inside the System: A Primer for Trustees," *Wilson Library Bulletin*, February 1986, 27-30.

GENERAL

Bird, Roy and Jana Renfro, comps. *Kansas Public Library Statistics— 1988*, Topeka, Kansas: The Library Development Division, Kansas State Library, 1989.

Covey, Steven R. *Seven Basic Habits of Highly Effective People*, Provo, Utah: Steven R. Covey and Associates, 1989. (Audio Cassette Seminar.)

Naisbitt, John. *Megatrends*. New York: Warner Books, 1984.

WRITING

Bates, Jefferson D. *Writing with Precision*. Rev. ed. Washington, D.C.: Acropolis Books, 1987.

Bradley, Jana and Larry. *Improving Written Communication in Libraries*. Chicago, London: American Library Association, 1988.

DuPont, M. Kay. *Don't Let Your Participles Dangle in Public*. Atlanta: DuPont and Disend, 1987.

Land, Myrick. *Writing for Magazines*. Englewood Cliffs, New Jersey: Prentice-Hall Inc. 1987.

Strunk, William, Jr. and E. B. White. *The Elements of Style*. 3rd ed. New York: Macmillan Publishing Company, 1979.

Zinsser, William. *On Writing Well*. 3rd ed. New York: Perennial Library, Harper and Row, 1988.

Zinsser, William. *Writing to Learn*. New York: Perennial Library, Harper and Row, 1989.

INDEX

WITHDRAWN